MAKING STANDARDS WORK

How to Implement Standards- Based Assessments in the Classroom, School, and District

DOUGLAS B. REEVES, Ph.D.

Center for Performance Assessment

Notice of Liability

ISBN #0-9644955-2-X

Edited by
Julee Brooke ▪ Donna Davis ▪ Kathi Lambert

Cover and publication design/layout by
Sherri Rowe ▪ sherrir@ruraltel.net ▪ (785) 425-7350

Printed and Bound in the United States of America

Published and Distributed by

Center for Performance Assessment
1660 South Albion Street ▪ Suite 1110 ▪ Denver, CO 80222
(303) 504-9312 ▪ 800-THINK-99 (800-844-6599) ▪ Fax: (303) 504-9417
Web Site: www.testdoctor.com ▪ E-mail: perfassess@aol.com

dedication

To:

Jean and Julie Reeves
who never lost faith

and

Brooks
who still makes me the luckiest father in the world.

about the author

Dr. Douglas B. Reeves is the Director of the Center for Performance Assessment^{SM}. He consults with school systems and universities throughout the world on issues relating to assessment, accountability, technology, and leadership. An innovator in the field of assessment and accountability systems, he is the author of six books and numerous articles. Dr. Reeves is in great demand as a speaker to educational, government, and business groups and has addressed audiences throughout the United States as well as in Asia, Africa, and Europe. As the "Test Doctor" of the Internet, he responds to questions from teachers, educational leaders, and students throughout the world as they seek information on the best practices in educational assessment, accountability, and leadership.

This book is the result of Dr. Reeves' work with literally hundreds of schools and thousands of teachers and administrators. Their questions and insistent demands to make performance assessment practical, relevant, and meaningful to the real world of today's students and educators form the foundation of this volume.

Acknowledgments

Every book is a collaborative process, and credit is due to many more people than the one whose name appears on the cover. In particular, I would like to thank my colleagues at the Center for Performance Assessment who have provided valuable critiques and suggestions. The thanks expressed here are insufficient recognition of their intellectual energy and friendship They are: Dr. Kurt Beerline, Dr. Julee Brooke, Donna Davis, Deborah Lagerborg, Kathi Lambert, Dr. Scott Marion, Lamech Mbioo, Dr Alan Moore, Dr. John Nordin, Dr. David B. Thomas, Gail Young.

This second edition of *Making Standards Work* reflects significant improvements and revisions from the first edition. I am especially grateful to a small group of hard working, dedicated individuals who provided substantial editing and technical assistance and contributed creative and intellectual insights to this edition. Special thanks are owed to Julee Brooke, Donna Davis, Kathi Lambert, and Gail Young. Julie Reeves painstakingly reviewed and edited the original manuscript for spelling, grammar, and coherence.

A number of leaders in the field of standards-based performance assessment have provided valuable insights and contributed to the ideas expressed herein. Dr. Henry Roman, Superintendent of Pueblo School District No. 60, provided an exceptional opportunity for me to watch effective standards implementation at close range. Dr. Joyce Bales, Dean of Education at the University of Southern Colorado, has been an innovator, colleague, and friend. Dr. Stan Scheer has forced me to temper my enthusiasm with the practicality that only a school superintendent can provide. Dr. Deanna Housfeld is a singularly effective educational leader whose demands for detail, practicality, and real world effectiveness set the standard by which every educator, consultant, and leader should be evaluated. Dr. Gerry George and Mrs. Kathy Gardner are innovators in the field of professional development whose conferences and satellite network programs allow state of the art ideas and best practices in education to be widely shared with educators, administrators, and policy makers throughout the world.

Students in my graduate research classes frequently hear the words that references must be cited, not simply because the style manual requires it, but because we have an ethical obligation to acknowledge the shoulders on which we stand. Five people in particular deserve this acknowledgment, for their writing and thinking have shaped much of my intellectual life. Howard Gardner, Ruth Mitchell, David Perkins, Robert Slavin, and Grant Wiggins have written cogently for a generation of teachers, educational leaders, and policy makers about the profound need for thinking about learning, intelligence, and achievement in new ways. They have elevated public debate from the exchange of labels and attribution of motives, an all too typical occurrence in the past, to a respectful dialogue about ideas and the imperative that the world has to better educate its children.

Finally, Professors Audrey Kleinsasser and Alan Moore have provided to me and countless other students just the right combination of encouragement, skepticism, good humor, and challenge. This expression of thanks is woefully inadequate.

As usual, this attempt to share credit does not constitute an attempt to share blame, and the mistakes, whether intellectual or typographical, are ones for which I alone bear responsibility.

Douglas Reeves
September, 1997

Contents

Part Three—Making Standards Work in the District

Part Four

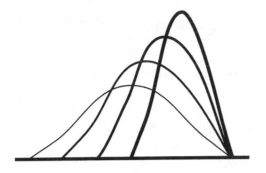

introduction

How to Get the Most Out of This Book

This volume is designed not simply to be read, but to be used. It is written principally for use by classroom teachers and administrators at the building and district level. However, many of those interested in effective educational strategies, including students of educational leadership and assessment, parents, board members, and policy makers may find this format useful.

■ Part One

Part One addresses why standards matter. The central rationale for standards-based assessments is that they provide a means of evaluation that is accurate and fair. An essential component of fairness is consistency—students and teachers have a fixed target at which to aim. In contrast to norm-referenced measures frequently in use by school districts, the standards-based academic target does not change.

If, for example, students are expected to demonstrate proficiency in the application of the Pythagorean theorem (Figure I.1, right) after a ninth grade geometry class, they can take scant comfort in being better than other students. Proficiency is more than beating other students. It is insufficient to be better than 50% of the other ninth graders in the nation by successfully answering—or guessing—the responses to a multiple choice test, and then claiming that one is "above average."

figure I.1

Pythagorean Theorem $a^2 + b^2 = c^2$

A standards-based system will require the student to demonstrate the application of the Pythagorean theorem—perhaps by using pencil and paper, perhaps by using blocks of wood, or perhaps by using a video-taped oral presentation. In none of these cases can a student guess the right answer. In this respect, standards-based assessments are inevitably more rigorous and more demanding than traditional multiple choice tests. Moreover, the requirement to demonstrate that the sum of the square of two sides of a right triangle is equal to the square of the hypotenuse ($a^2 + b^2 = c^2$) does not change, while the national average does change from year to year. Part One will address why this method of assessment is the appropriate way to implement standards and what the roles of classroom teachers, principals, and district officials are with respect to implementing such a system.

■ Part Two

Part Two of this book addresses, in a step-by-step manner, the process of making standards work in the classroom. All too frequently, the model of educational innovation has been that of a single teacher who attends a workshop, comes back to school full of innovative ideas and enthusiasm, and implements those ideas—in one classroom. Sometimes, though rarely, these ideas are shared with others. Even more rarely are they implemented by others. But on the whole, innovation is sporadic and inconsistent.

The process of implementing standards-based performance assessments, by contrast, demands a collegial effort. The requirement for collegiality is not merely a social or political necessity. Effective assessments require consistent evaluation and the application of several disciplines at the same time. If a school system has a writing standard, for example, and teachers create assessments in mathematics, science, and social studies without regard for the writing standards, chaos ensues. Students recognize these inconsistencies and will be the first to tell us that the standards emperor has no clothes. If, on the other hand, standards are consistently applied in assessments in which the evaluation criteria do not change from one discipline to the next, student performance responds accordingly. Such a move from idiosyncrasy to consistency requires cooperative work by teachers. Only with this consistency will policy makers, taxpayers and, most importantly, students, understand that standards have moved from slogans and speeches to clear and unambiguous practice in the classroom.

The issue of consistency invariably raises the issue of teacher independence and discretion. Let us not mince words here: in few other professions do practitioners of all levels of experience and education have such broad discretion to make critical decisions throughout the vast majority of the day. The adoption of standards, consistently applied through standards-based performance assessments, retains large amounts of this discretion, freedom, and individual judgment. But this freedom has limits. The widespread practice of teachers defining curriculum and choosing not to teach critical subjects based on little more than their personal preference will, in a standards-based school system, go the way of the Dodo bird. Changes in teaching practice and experiments in learning activities are one thing; choosing to omit fractions for a third grade class because, in the words of one teacher, "I don't like fractions," is an intolerable abuse of discretion.

The need for consistency in the application of standards is based on more than a bureaucratic imperative for control or the psychometric zeal for statistical reliability. Consistency is required by our commitment to fairness. Any reasonable notion of fairness requires that educational strategies, particularly assessments, must be consistent within a school system. This means, as a practical matter, that "spelling counts" in math class as surely as it does in an English class. It implies that "math counts" in a graph provided to the social studies or economics teacher as surely as it does were the graph submitted to the science or math teacher. Although the development of standards-based performance assessments permits an extraordinary amount of creativity by individual teachers, the standards themselves remain fixed guiding stars by which educators and administrators can navigate.

The Ten Steps described in Part Two comprise the heart of this book. The application of these steps to a single assignment and single standard by every teacher in a district can, over the course of two to three years, completely change the way educational strategies are developed, delivered, and assessed.

■ Part Three

Part Three addresses the broader policy issues involved when making standards work in the district. Accountability, recognition, and response to challenges are among the critical issues of this section of the book. These chapters offer concrete and specific ideas helpful to superintendents and other educational leaders at the district level.

■ Part Four

Finally, the reader will find reproducible handouts for easy review of key information, detailed sample assessments and assignments (including a sample format for assignments), a handy glossary, and a brief bibliography. School reform does not take place with books or speeches. School reform takes place through the actions of individual parents, teachers, and administrators who are willing to change what happens in the classroom. The standards movement can have an enormous influence on a national commitment to excellence and equity, but it will inherently be the culmination of the efforts of teachers and school leaders working together, rather than a march in lock-step fashion to a uniform drumbeat. At the Center for Performance Assessment, we continue to gather stories of successful and unsuccessful innovations, and we hope that you might take a moment to share your stories with us. We look forward to an engaging, challenging dialogue with each of our readers and encourage you to contact us.

Center for Performance Assessment
1660 South Albion Street ▪ Suite 1110 ▪ Denver, CO 80222
(303) 504-9312 ▪ 800-THINK-99 (800-844-6599) ▪ Fax: (303) 504-9417
Web Site: www.testdoctor.com ▪ E-mail: perfassess@aol.com

PART ONE

Why

Standards

Matter

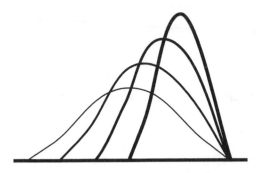

chapter one

Tying the Bell on the Cat

The implementation of standards brings to mind this classic fairy tale.

> **O**nce upon a time a council of mice gathered to consider how to deal with their deadly enemy, the cat. After much deliberation, the council decided that the best thing to do would be to tie a bell around the neck of the cat so that the mice would be warned whenever the cat approached. Amidst their general back slapping and self-congratulation, a small young voice uttered the telling question, "But who will tie the bell on the cat?"

This book is about "tying the bell on the cat." The national standards movement now faces a similar dilemma. There appears to be general agreement across the political spectrum that academic standards should:

- Be rigorous and challenging

- Be related to the technological forces that will mold the twenty-first century in which today's students will work

- Provide a fair and equitable basis for evaluation

However, there is widespread and deep disagreement about how schools will be held accountable for the implementation of these standards. Without accountability and without comprehensive and meaningful assessments, the standards movement contains little more than platitudes. While high expectations are certainly an important part of successful academic achievement strategies, expectations alone are insufficient. Assessment and accountability drive every other element of the education delivery system, including instructional design, classroom technique, allocation of resources, administrative practice, and central office decision making.

■ Linking Standards to Assessments—An International Challenge

This issue crosses national boundaries. In August of 1997, I addressed a policy roundtable at the International Conference on Technology and Education in Oslo, Norway. Representatives of 57 countries heard speeches from leaders including a Prime Minister, several cabinet-level education officials, and a large number of leaders from universities and school systems. They appeared to be united on the necessity for high standards and placed particular emphasis on the need for technology literacy, student collaboration, and "higher order thinking skills." The most frequent comment from the delegates of the many nations was, "The same speech could have been delivered by educational leaders in our country." I then asked the group a simple question: if there is such unanimity on the need for high standards in thinking skills, collaborative work, and technology literacy, can any of the 57 nations here claim to have an assessment system that reflects these philosophies? In fact, can any nation claim to have an assessment system that doesn't reflect the opposite of what we claim to believe? One American community college dean said that they required technology performance assessment. A few delegates said that they were experimenting with individual proficiency tests at the university level.

These noble efforts notwithstanding, the state of assessment is now little different than it has been for decades. School leaders and national policy makers talk about laudatory goals, and then continue to use tests that discourage (or more likely, prohibit) teamwork, cooperation and collaboration. The most frequently used tests encourage memorization of narrowly defined fact patterns or vocabulary words, and rarely require students to explain or justify their answers, analyze and synthesize information, or apply general principles to new and unfamiliar information. These are the skills required in the never-never land of political speeches, but rarely assessed in the classroom.

■ The Central Issue: How To Make Standards Work

Despite this discouraging reality, the voices demanding change are gaining national and international attention. As far as voters and most board of education members are concerned, the issue is not whether to create effective accountability and assessment, but how to do it. There are a few hold-outs remaining who regard accountability and assessment as inherently improper, unfair, demeaning, and even unprofessional, but these voices are rarely taken seriously in most debates over educational policy. The new voices in the debate demand accountability and assessment systems that are based on high academic standards and that reflect the consensus of their communities about what students should know and be able to do. These voices lack the patience to debate endlessly whether we should have effective assessment—they demand to know how to implement effective assessment. It is to these energetic, innovative and—yes—frustrated voices that this book is addressed. Their central question is: now that we have standards, how do we make them work?

■ What Makes the Standards Approach Different From Business As Usual?

Many school systems across the United States and abroad have endured the arduous process of establishing academic standards. This has been no easy task, particularly in the politically charged areas of social studies, economics, and literature. As difficult as these tasks have been, however, even more difficulty lies ahead when transforming standards into assessments. If standards are to be successfully implemented, then many of the traditional ways of doing things must cease.

Examples of traditional activities that can no longer take place under a standards-driven environment include the following:

- **Attendance (or "seat time") is sufficient to gain credit.**

  This issue frequently leads to a debate over "social promotion" versus "high standards," with the implication that high standards invariably lead to flunking students. In fact, high standards are founded on the core belief that all students can perform at high levels given the opportunity to learn, and with appropriate teaching and assessment strategies. Therefore, the practical impact of the application of high standards is neither high failure rates nor social promotion—it is rather the use of multiple opportunities for students to demonstrate proficiency, and the steadfast refusal of teachers and administrators to label a student as "proficient" when they are not.

- **A "D" is a passing grade.**

  I know of no classroom in America in which a "D" represents anything other than the failure of the student to demonstrate proficiency and the failure of the teacher to acknowledge it. The availability of a "D" is simply the policy option that allows a school to explicitly acknowledge that a student failed to demonstrate proficiency in the subject, while refusing to require the student to do so. In a genuinely standards-based school system, the grade of "D" should not exist. Either students are proficient (usually a grade of at least an "A" or "B" and, sometimes, a "C") or they are not. The failure to be proficient should, in most circumstances, result in a grade of "incomplete" while the student is afforded more opportunities to learn and demonstrate proficiency. Should the student refuse to do so, a failing grade, not a "D," is the only accurate grade.

- **A great high school is measured by the quantity and creativity of its elective offerings.**

  There is not a shred of evidence to suggest that the proliferation of non-academic electives have improved student learning. But there is a growing quantity of statistical and narrative evidence that an emphasis on core academic disciplines promotes student learning, not only in traditional test scores, but also in complex performance assessments. Nevertheless, there are hundreds of high schools that have academic standards for statistics and economics, but offer no classes in these subjects, while the same schools devote time and resources to classes for which the community has no academic standards. **Note well:** this does not make a brief for a curriculum based only on the "three R's" but rather insists that every class, regardless of its label, owes a duty to the student and community to reinforce academic standards in math, language arts, social studies, and science. Classes in music, cooking, wood shop, and physical education offer extraordinary opportunities to teach math, science, history, and language arts. We cannot squander the talents and time of these teachers, nor can we afford the inconsistent message that such subjects are "soft" because they are not really academic. The defensiveness of teachers (and more commonly, some professional associations) on the subject of academic emphasis in elective subjects is misplaced.

- **Academic core curriculum classes are identical in structure and length for every student.**

  The common practice requiring that every ninth grade student should take the identical math class (typical algebra) is absurd. In a diverse district (that is, any district without a small and neatly identical group of students), some students come to the ninth grade ready for trigonometry while others require basic mathematical skills in order to avoid a catastrophic failure. Some students are ready for the challenges of literary criticism and advanced composition, while others need work on the funda-mentals of spelling and grammar. A standards-based approach to education begins with the premise that all students can learn and achieve at high levels—*but that does not imply that all students learn in the same way and at the same pace*. Standards-based districts expect that all students will achieve—that does not mean that they should expect that all students will learn in the identical manner and at the same pace. The practical impact of standards implementation is more than a series of community meetings in which everyone exclaims how nice it would be if all students learned math, English, history, and technology. This will remain the stuff of Rotary Club lunch speeches unless it is transformed into specific curriculum reforms.

It is likely that many school districts that began establishing standards would never have completed the journey had they realized that the elimination of these notions are the practical outcome of standards implementation. A standards-driven district, however, cannot afford the luxury of paying lip service to academic standards by implementing a system based only upon attendance (or "seat time"), hourly credit, and ancient definitions of satisfactory. Let us consider each of these implications in some detail.

■ It's Proficiency—Not Seat Time—That Matters

Standards implementation depends on a demonstration of proficiency. Traditional means of assessment, such as a letter grade associated with "seat time," are hardly ever an indication that a student has met standards. Indeed, most teachers would agree that students to whom they have given a "D" grade do not meet the standards for that class, and the teacher would have regarded the "D" as an unsatisfactory grade. Nevertheless, for the purposes of awarding the ultimate credit—a high school diploma—the "D" is regarded as satisfactory.

If standards mean anything, they mean that students must demonstrate proficiency in order to obtain credit for classes and, ultimately, in order to obtain a high school diploma from that school system. This means that the era of credit for attendance and class participation is over. Students gain credit through a demonstration of proficiency. This can be done either at the beginning of the class, in the middle of the class, or at the end of class. For students who demonstrate proficiency early, the classroom teacher has the responsibility of providing enrichment opportunities that allow those students to indicate that they have exceeded standards. For students who have difficulty achieving standards, the teacher has the obligation to provide multiple opportunities for those students to make progress towards standards and, ultimately, to meet the standards. For students who, at the end of the term, fail to meet standards, the teacher has an obligation to forthrightly indicate that the student does not meet standards, and hence was awarded no credit for the achievement of that standard. Along with this obligation to tell the uncomfortable truth, teachers have the obligation to continue to help the student work toward the achievement of that standard.

■ Standards Lead to Curriculum Reform

Standards implementation inevitably leads to curriculum reform, including the provision of intensive assistance for small groups of students who are not initially meeting standards. Another essential element of curriculum reform is the systematic use of standards in the description of courses. At the very least, this means that every class (particularly in a middle school, junior high, or high school) is listed in a course catalog and is associated with one or more standards established by the district. Some districts, for example, have standards in statistics, but no classes in it. On the other hand, they have classes in psychology, sociology, and photography, but no standards are associated with those classes.

If standards are to become more than a slogan, then one of two things must happen. Either the classes that are not associated with standards are no longer taught, or—a better alternative—the teachers of those classes creatively identify ways their classes can help students achieve academic standards. For example, statistics standards can clearly be met in a number of sociology, ethnic studies, psychology, and social studies classes. The same is true of many language arts and civics standards. The photography class could be linked to standards in mathematics, language arts, and civics. The bottom line remains, however, that classes not linked to standards do not make a contribution to the goals of the district and should not be taught.

Standards implementation requires a compartmentalized curriculum. By compartmentalization, I mean the reduction of some academic subjects into smaller blocks. There should be no such thing as "ninth grade mathematics" or "tenth grade English." Rather, standards that these classes have traditionally comprised should be taught in units ranging in size from a few weeks to a full semester. It might be possible that some students would take two classes to complete all those requirements—the time traditionally used for a full class. Other students, however, may need four, five, or even six units to achieve the same level of standards.

This is most evident in mathematics classes. The notion that every ninth and tenth grader should take the same algebra class is simply preposterous. A number of students enter high school without knowing multiplication tables, not to mention having any preparation for algebra class. The traditional system requires that these students take a class for which they are hopelessly ill-prepared and then brands those students as failures in mathematics. A better approach is to permit these students to achieve high school mathematics standards through a number of different classes, including not only traditional academic classes, but also application classes, vocational classes, and interdisciplinary classes. Those students still have to achieve the algebra standard but they do so by taking a variety of classes—not by taking a "dumbed-down" curriculum.

The goal of a standards-based curriculum is not to tell students how to achieve standards, but rather to provide a broad menu of alternatives that meet the needs of students who require additional instruction, as well as those who have already achieved the standard and appreciate further enrichment. The practical effect of this system is that students who need to spend more class time to accomplish the graduation standards will take fewer electives. Does this mean that a student who needs extra math and English classes in order to achieve high school graduation might not have time in his or her curriculum for band and drama? That is precisely what it means. This leads to the next issue. Standards implementation almost invariably implies fewer electives.

■ What About "Non-Academic" Electives?

One of the many ill-considered trends in secondary school education in the last twenty years has been the proliferation of non-academic electives. Although many of these classes have earned high marks for innovation and creativity, they have done little to contribute to the academic achievement of students. Even in districts that claim to be standards-based, many of these electives continue to thrive in ignorant bliss of any responsibility the teachers of these electives should have with regard to standards implementation. Although I acknowledge the social importance of many electives, these are times of limited resources and falling academic achievement in many districts. Such times call for making choices with regard to available time and resources. Although it may not be necessary to eliminate electives in instrumental music, chorus, journalism, drama, social sciences, and creative writing (just to name a few), it is essential that these electives be available only to students who have already achieved the standards appropriate for their grade level, or that those classes are directly used to help all students achieve academic standards. In addition, the teachers of these elective subjects bear a responsibility for either demonstrating that their classes can, in fact, help students achieve specific academic standards, or accepting the fact that the activities in which they are engaged are more appropriate as after-school extracurricular activities. To be sure, there are a number of teachers of music, shop, home economics, and many other electives who can be splendid mathematics and English teachers if only given the chance to use these subjects, which they so creatively teach, to help students achieve academic standards.

There is substantial controversy on the subject of whether "non-academic" subjects should have their own standards. This position is advocated by many professional groups associated with music, physical education, and vocational education. They argue separate standards makes these subjects part of the standards movement. In my view, such a movement is precisely wrong. It distances these subjects from core academic subjects and may doom them to irrelevance. A better approach is to integrate these traditionally "non-academic" subjects with academic standards. For example, woodworking and cooking become ways to teach math and science. Music and art become ways to teach history and literature. This integration will elevate the status of music, art, woodworking, home economics, and subjects that are too frequently placed on the chopping block during budget difficulties. In sum, the importance of these subjects is best recognized, not by their isolation, but by their integration into the core academic content standards of our schools.

Standards and High School Graduation Requirements

Standards implementation implies different graduation requirements. The myth of the "gentleman's C" (or given today's grade inflation, the "gentleman's A–") holds that mere attendance without an excess of disruptive behavior qualifies a student for a passing grade in a class. If standards are to have meaning, then a demonstration of proficiency must be linked to the awarding of high school diplomas. Many progressive districts are moving toward a certificate of completion for students who have been able to pass the attendance requirements for graduation but were unable to demonstrate proficiency in academic standards after the normal number of high school years. Typically, these students are offered a fifth year of instruction, at no charge, either in the secondary school setting or in an appropriate post-secondary institution.

Standards Call for Courage

For most, "tying the bell on the cat" requires courage, just as it did for the council of mice. Districts that seek to undertake standards must be prepared to face the political firestorm that accompanies a restriction on student choices and a diminution of the widespread emphasis on non-academic elective subjects. Moreover, criticism will inevitably come from those who believe the application of curriculum blocks is too close to "tracking." As a result, they will brand the implementation of standards as unfair, sexist, racist, and other appellations that say more about the level of educational and political discourse than they do about the targets of the labels.

Finally, criticism will come from teachers, themselves, who appreciate performance-based assessments of standards in theory, but who are less than enthusiastic when they discover that the primary responsibility for the creation and year-round administration of these assessments rests with the classroom teacher. Only those districts willing to risk the wrath of all of these criticisms, and many more, are going to be able to successfully implement standards. The result will certainly be worth it in academic achievement, fairness, equity, educational opportunity, professional development for teachers, public accountability, and in many other ways. But only the most innovative and courageous districts will endure the pain and discomfort of these criticisms in order to achieve those long-term results.

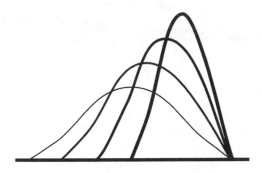

chapter two

Getting to Know Your Standards

"We've been working on standards for three years, and I still don't know what they mean."

These sentiments, expressed by teachers, administrators, parents, and board members, grow largely from the failure of the advocates of standards to be precise in their language. This chapter addresses some of the causes of this confusion and suggests a means to bring some order to the chaos that frequently surrounds the discussion of school standards.

Most readers of this volume will already have adopted some sort of academic standards. If your district has not yet started this process, or if you remain in the midst of the standards-setting process, an excellent guide has been recently published by The Education Trust in Washington, D.C. The volume is called *Front-End Alignment: Using Standards to Steer Educational Change* by Dr. Ruth Mitchell, one of the leading authors in the standards movement.[1] This is a short, practical guide that will help working groups quickly get to the point and achieve their objectives. Among the more important contributions that Dr. Mitchell has made to the standards discussion is a clarification of terminology.

Unfortunately, the term standards means vastly different things to different people. In some school systems, standards describe general expectations for student knowledge, while in

---

1. Ruth Mitchell, *Front-End Alignment: Using Standards to Steer Education Change—A Manual for Developing Standards*. (Washington, D.C.: The Education Trust, 1996), pp. 4-5. To order, contact: Publications Orders Desk, American Association for Higher Education, One Dupont Circle, NW, Suite 360, Washington, D.C., 20036-1110, Telephone 202-293-6440, ext. 11, Fax 202-293-0073.

others, standards describe very specific performance requirements. When the same word—"standards"—is used to describe very different things, some confusion and frustration is inevitable.

After working with hundreds of schools on this subject, I am convinced that the use of the word "standards" to mean many different things is confusing and potentially destructive. Therefore let me suggest vocabulary that will be clear and unambiguous:

- *Academic Content Standards*—The general expectations of what a student should know and be able to do. These are typically few in number and general in scope. Examples include:

  - Students will be able to design, conduct, analyze, evaluate, and communicate about scientific investigations.

  - Students will know and understand properties, forms, changes in, and inter-relationship of matter and energy.

  - Students will communicate clearly and effectively about science to others.

- *Benchmarks*—The specific expectations of student performance at critical levels of school, typically fourth, eighth, and twelfth grades.

  - By Grade 4, students will identify and describe science related problems or issues, such as acid rain and weather forecasting.

  - By Grade 4, students will relate science information to local and global issues, such as world hunger and ozone depletion.

  - By Grade 8, students will analyze the risks and benefits of potential solutions to personal and global issues.

  - By Grade 12, students will analyze the costs, risks, benefits, and consequences of natural resource exploration, development, and consumption, such as resource management of forests and ground water pollution.

  - By Grade 12, students will design, communicate, and, when possible, implement solutions to personal, social, and global problems, such as school noise pollution or school recycling.

- *Scoring Guides*—These are the very specific descriptions of student proficiency for an individual standards-based assessment. For example:

    – To earn a score of "proficient," the student will produce an informative essay with no spelling, grammar, or punctuation errors. The essay will be accompanied by at least two graphs that include data points and relationships that support the conclusions of the essay. The graphs will be mathematically accurate, properly labeled, and clearly related to the essay. (**Note:** Students will have at least three opportunities to submit work, make changes, and re-submit it in their pursuit of a score of "proficient.")

figure 2.1

Standards Vocabulary

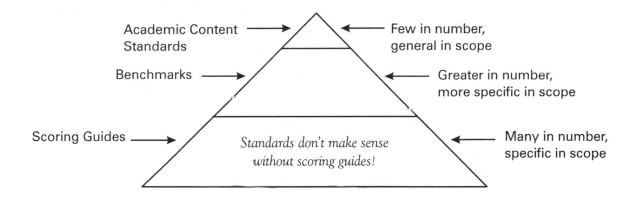

The Relationship Between Standards, Benchmarks, and Scoring Guides

Figure 2.1 illustrates the relationship between scoring guides, benchmarks, and academic content standards. It might take several different assessments, and hence several different scoring guides for a student to demonstrate that she has achieved a benchmark. It will take several different benchmarks—all completed with proficient performance—for a student to demonstrate that she has achieved an academic content standard.

Vocabulary is Important

These recommendations for standards vocabulary omit some commonly used words. Rather than "rubrics"—educational jargon centuries old—use the term "scoring guide." Rather than using the word "standards" with different descriptions, use the complete phrase "academic content standards." This helps to clearly differentiate them from "outcomes based education."

Although that philosophy was born of good intentions, its final implementation sometimes appeared to be more related to how students "think and feel" than to what students "can know and do." The latter is the essence of "academic content standards" and the distinction from outcomes based education is a critical one for many parents and board members.

If you have not already done so, please take time to become familiar with the standards in your state and district. It simply does not make sense for schools to "reinvent the wheel" when a significant amount of effort has already gone into the process of developing academic content standards. Moreover, many states require that districts establish standards at least as challenging as those adopted at the state level. Therefore, it is imperative that educators, administrators, and policy-makers take some time to become familiar with their state academic content standards.

■ Where Do I Start?

The academic standards can appear to be overwhelming at first glance. After all, they represent the collective efforts of your community or your state to articulate what students should learn. Many teachers and parents initially respond, "I'm swamped with work already—how can they expect me to do all this stuff too?" The rule, when confronted with such a large body of information, is "one handful of mud at a time." Start with a content area with which you are comfortable, and then look at the description of the standards for one area within that field.

■ Why Are Standards for Several Grades Mixed Together?

One of the first things you will notice as you get to know your standards is that they are mixed in groups of grades. There are usually three such groups: kindergarten through fourth grades, fifth through eighth grades, and ninth through twelfth grades. Many people looking at standards for the first time find this baffling—how can you expect a third grade student to be doing the same work as a first grade student? The reason is that our traditional groupings of children into grades has been a reflection of our need for order and convenience more than it has been a reflection of how children learn and behave. In fact, it is quite common for a single classroom in a primary grade to have children who are working below, at, and above the level traditionally associated with that grade. The standards, when described for a group of grades, acknowledge that we must address a continuum of learning covering many different activities, not just traditional grades and not just an isolated set of skills traditionally associated with a single age or grade.

■ Standards Are Concerned With the Reality of Student Achievement—Not Artificial and Meaningless Time Requirements

The traditional approach has held that children have a fixed amount of time to learn something and assumes that the learning will be variable. For example, "You learn to add and subtract in first grade—but let's face it, some kids just won't make it." A nation that expects to have its children compete in the twenty-first century can ill-afford such a primitive and unrealistic approach to education. In fact, the learning expectation must be fixed—children will learn to add and subtract. The time it takes to learn this may be shorter for some children and longer for others, but it is not acceptable that "some kids just won't learn it." At the very heart of the standards movement is the change from fixed time, variable learning, to variable amounts of time to learn with fixed standards for learning. Standards-based districts understand that some students will learn to read in one year, while others may need three years. They understand that some ninth grade students can complete algebra in six months, while others may need two years. Standards-based districts are committed to the principle that all of their students will read, and that all of their ninth grade students will learn algebra. These school systems care about achievement—not about time requirements of a bygone era. Chapter 3 will provide greater elaboration on this important concept.

■ Translating Standards Into Activities

Let us consider a sample content standard:

> Students will relate physical materials, pictures, and diagrams to mathematical ideas.

Whatever your mathematical background, you can imagine some ways students can demonstrate that they meet this standard. For a student in the early grades, this might include working and playing with blocks and creating some elementary mathematical relationships with them. For older students, this might include drawing pictures of a house and calculating the dimensions of their drawings. The point is that students demonstrate that they have met this standard not by responding to artificial (and boring!) multiple choice questions involving pictures and mathematical concepts, but by engaging in realistic, interesting, and thought-provoking activities.

Obviously, there is much more to the creation of standards-based performance assignments than we have described here. The entire process includes the development of a scoring guide, several rounds of critiques by colleagues and students, and the deliberate inclusion of other disciplines into the exercise so that each assignment is a rich tapestry of different activities. Part Two of this book deals at length with the creation of standards-based performance assignments and Part Four provides several illustrations of how standards can come to life.

■ What Happens if Students Do Not Meet the Standards?

This is perhaps the question most frequently asked by parents, teachers, and administrators. "Some kids just don't get it," they argue. It would be more precise to say, "Using our present methods of instruction and our present notions of curriculum and grades, some kids don't have much of a chance to 'get it'." The straight answer to the question of, "What happens if students don't meet the standards?" is that the student does the assignment again or has additional opportunities in other contexts to meet the standards. Indeed, revision and improvement is one of the distinguishing features of a standards-based performance assignment. It is not a "one shot" ordeal.

■ From "Saturday Night Specials" to Continuous Improvement

In the traditional model, students have one shot at performance—the typical final exam. But in real life, we are constantly working on problems, making modifications, improving our work, and then examining it to see if it meets the needs of our colleagues or if it needs yet more improvement. Far better work is done in college (and I would argue, in business) by students who are used to the process of continuous improvement than by those who have been conditioned to make every project a "Saturday night special" with one attempt at perfection and without the process of revision, reflection, and improvement.

■ Grading and Standards

In the traditional model, the price of not meeting the standard has been a "D–" (or with today's grade inflation, perhaps a "C" or a "B–"). These marks tell the parents, "This student really can't do the work, but I'm not going to go through the political hassles associated with holding the child back a year or getting sued. Hey, he's really unsatisfactory, but let's call it passing." Sometimes this is done under the mistaken notion of building a student's self-esteem. In fact, there is only one thing to call such a practice, and that is a lie, and a particularly destructive lie, too. The worst damage done to a student's self-esteem is not when she is told that she does not meet a standard. Rather, it is when she finds out that although through all the years of school her teachers told her that she could "get by," now her prospective employers, college professors, professional licensing boards, and others who are the gatekeepers for her opportunities in the future, are all telling her that she can no longer succeed.

How do we break this cycle of deceit? How do we stop lying to children when we tell them that they are meeting standards when, in fact, it is manifestly clear that they are not meeting the standard? One of the principal advantages of the standards-based approach is that it begins with the premise that all children can learn. This is not an empty slogan, but a fact. Given sufficient time and attention, every student can meet standards. Contemporary educators have much to learn in this respect from the discipline of special education. Here, a generation of teachers using a methodical, interdisciplinary, standards-based approach has demonstrated, in literally thousands of cases, that children on whom the traditional educational system had given up were able to learn, and to learn at high levels.

■ What Do We Do When Students Don't Meet Standards?

In practical terms, this means that when children first attempt a standards-based assignment and fail to meet the standards, they are not given a low grade and then pushed onto the next assignment. Rather, they revise their work and submit it again, and again, and again. In a classroom in which standards are clearly ingrained into the students' learning behaviors, it is not unusual to see a child on the way to the teacher's desk and then, noticing the standard on the bulletin board, stop, return to the desk, and make an important revision. This is the process we wish to encourage in our writers, engineers, scientists, accountants, attorneys, and, one might hope, teachers and professors.

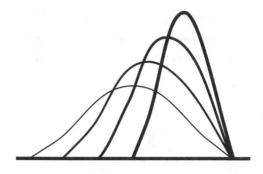

chapter three

Standards and Norms— What is the Difference?

"I've already got high standards in my class—only a few get an 'A' and more than 40 percent can't pass!"

— Ninth grade math teacher

At the very core of the standards movement is the notion that student achievement is measured against a fixed indicator, not against other students. While this may seem obvious, this issue is at the heart of resistance to the standards movement. School officials, board members, teachers, and parents who have been exposed to standards and expressed their hearty approval of them will nevertheless ask the question, "But, how are the students doing compared to the average?" In a district genuinely committed to standards-based achievement, the answer is, "We don't know, and we don't care."

This chapter outlines the differences between standards and norms as the reference for student achievement, and highlights the reasons this distinction is critical to the understanding and implementation of a successful standards-based education program. The following differences are paramount.

■ Standards Are Fixed. Norms Move.

Consider a mathematical standard in which students are expected to "find the area of a triangle." In a standards-based system, the student has not achieved the standard until she can successfully determine the area of a triangle. If a student is able to accomplish the task successfully, along with the vast majority of other students in the class, that one student is not heaped in the middle of a distribution and labeled as the "fiftieth percentile." Rather, the student has achieved the standard. This is the only thing that matters.

Consider the situation in which there is only one student in the class who is progressing toward the standard, but still has not achieved proficiency in that standard. The other students are not progressing toward the standard. The one student who is making progress toward the standard should not be recognized as achieving the ninety-ninth percentile with all the glory and honor associated with such an exalted position. Rather, that student, along with all the students in that class, has not yet met the standard and every single one of them needs additional work to achieve the standard.

The norm may change from year to year as testing companies publish data with different numbers of "average" achievement by students, but the standard—to add, subtract, multiply, divide, and (in the present case) find the area of geometric shapes—does not change. It would, after all, be scant comfort to an engineering company (and to the tenants of the building which that engineering company might construct) if its newest hire were unable to properly calculate the load-bearing ability of the parking lot, but the engineer was proudly able to say "but my math abilities are better than those of most of my peers!" In the real world we are much less interested in how people fare relative to one another. What matters is only the central question, can they do the job?

■ Standards Are Cooperative. Norms Are Competitive.

My observation of students in graduate and professional schools across the country would indicate that not much has changed in twenty-five years. The movie *The Paper Chase* illustrates the insidious nature of competition among first year law students. In the movie, students who have compiled outlines that will assist them in taking their final exams are unwilling to give them to other students unless they can gain something back of equal value. After all, they reason, there will be only one top A in the class, and there will only be a fixed number of people in the top ten percent—the only thing that matters in the mind-set of these students.

It has never been clear to me why employers insist on hiring the "top graduates," and thereby perpetuate such a competitive atmosphere. Then the employers wonder why the bright young people they hire might have a difficult time fulfilling their expected role as "team player." The senior partners in such firms appear to expect a personality change from the rapacious to the cooperative with the stroke of a pen. Unfortunately, the lessons of competition and avarice so long in gestation are difficult to eradicate.

In a standards-based educational system, the first year law students would need to know the elements of a contract. There may be a number of opportunities to distinguish themselves— writing law review articles, participating in moot court competitions, and perhaps even helping other students master the intricacies of contract law. However, the evaluation of a student's proficiency in a course on contracts would be determined by whether or not the students could, given a typical law school final exam scenario, identify the elements of the contract, whether it is enforceable, and what its strengths and weaknesses might be. Students are not graded along a continuum of how well they do compared to each other, but on whether or not they can analyze the contract. If they cannot, they must, as Professor Kingsfield said in *The Paper Chase*, "Take a dime, call your mother, and tell her you will not be a lawyer after all." If, on the other hand, students have demonstrated their mastery of contracts, then the exercise of distinguishing one student from the other based on arcane and meaningless distinctions is of no value to students, professors, employers, or the clients.

Perhaps the best models for measurement of performance against a standard are the training programs for our most delicate surgical specialties. When one is certified as a brain surgeon, there is not much differentiation between the top ten percent and the bottom ten percent. If a physician has such a certification and is ready to put a knife in the skull of his or her patients, then the patients have a right to assume the physician has met the standard and is competent. The competition among brain surgeons is of tiny consequence compared to the fundamental issue of whether or not the physician is competent to wield the knife. If that is the standard we apply to brain surgeons, pilots of airplanes, and most people in highly sensitive and demanding jobs, then why should not the same high standards be applied to mathematicians in middle school?

■ Standards Measure Proficiency. Norms and Their Counterparts (Grades) Measure Behavior.

Norms typically are identified by either the subjective opinions of teachers or the pseudo-objectivity of multiple choice tests, and they are a classic example of distinctions without a difference. More crudely, they are wild guesses carried out to three decimal points. The notion that, after four years of education, a 3.9 GPA (Grade Point Average) is "better" than a 3.85 GPA is ludicrous. And yet what student with a 3.9 GPA would stop for a moment to conduct a test of significance, demonstrating that the difference between 3.85 and 3.9 is very likely due to random variation and hence is not a meaningful or "statistically significant" difference?

■ Distinctions Without a Difference

Of course, we make the same silly distinctions all the time. We believe the Fortune 500 is a meaningful group, not thinking for a moment that it is indistinguishable from the Fortune 501 to any observer except, perhaps, the president of the 501st company on the list. The three best runners in the world receive medals in the Olympics, but the fourth best runner in the world is regarded as a loser.

For centuries we have bred a bone-deep belief that competition has intrinsic meaning and value. Certainly there is nothing wrong with competition. It is fun to watch. It is fun to be a participant. One can even argue that the winners of such competitions create appropriate role models for children. But even if all of these premises were accepted as true, it does not logically follow that the competitive model is appropriate for the educational setting.

■ The Game of Education is More than Individual Skill

Education is in actual practice much less like the Olympics than all-star wrestling. Without conducting a detailed journalistic inquiry into the nature of all-star wrestling, some observers might conclude that there are other factors at work in the determination of the victor apart from the athletic prowess of the victor. These include the competency of the manager, the cheering of the people at ringside, the prowess of one's teammate, one's experience in the genre, the script, and of course, the expectations of the crowd. All of these factors and others are at work in the competitive model of education. When defeating one's colleagues is not the primary goal, a remarkable thing happens. Whether it is solving a geometry problem or building muscle mass, when achievement of standards becomes the objective, participants accomplish more.

■ Cooperation Works

In a recent (1997) comprehensive review of research on educational innovations, Ellis and Fouts[2] found that the one innovation with the most clear and unambiguous link to improved student achievement was the use of cooperative learning. The nation's premier researcher of cooperative learning effects is Robert Slavin of Johns Hopkins University. It is important to note that Slavin's models of cooperative learning are not the ambiguous and ill-defined practices that frequently bear the label of "cooperation"—as if anything without a teacher's supervision deserved that label. In fact, structured cooperative learning groups insure that all students have the opportunity to assume different responsibilities and learn all aspects of solving a particular problem. Slavin's research is rigorous in linking cooperative learning techniques to individual performance and thus provides the best of all worlds—team skills, cooperative behavior, and individual results. The unfortunate conception that "cooperative learning" is the 1960s educational equivalent of "peace and free love" in the classroom makes for entertaining criticism, but doesn't square with the facts. The cooperative learning that Ellis, Fouts, Slavin and many others have studied leads to rigor and realism. Most importantly, it produces better mathematicians and writers than does a system based on competition.

■ Plato Was Wrong

In his *Republic*, Plato advocated a system of classification based upon "men of gold, men of silver, and men of bronze." Not surprisingly, philosophers such as Plato and his ilk were in the first category—men of gold. Lest any men of bronze wished to challenge the men of gold for their right to rule, such a notion would be easily scuttled by systematically denying to the men of bronze opportunities to succeed by limiting their access to everything from nutrition and housing to education. The supporters of a competitive model of education are, by and large, the modern day men of gold. The competitive system is less designed to challenge students, as its proponents claim, than it is to ensure a perpetuation of the caste system as it presently exists.

---

2. Ellis, A.K. & Fouts, J.T. (1997). *Research on educational innovations* (2nd ed.). Larchmont, NY: Eye on Education.

■ What We Can Learn from Athletic Standards

It is not coincidental that in our most standards-based endeavors—athletics, where the benchmarks are clear and the standards widely understood—the barriers of race and socioeconomic status have been most easily broken. Readers may question the word "easily." Although the athletes' abilities were there, the struggle remained to break the barrier of acceptance. But in the final analysis, spectators wanted to know to what degree Jesse Owens or Jackie Robinson could excel within a single-minded evaluation system based on the achievement of athletic standards. If, on the other hand, competition in a variety of skills, given the misnomer of intelligence, had been used for entry into Olympic competition or major league sports, those domains would be virtually segregated. Differences in exam performance do not occur because race or socioeconomic status are determiners of intelligence. These imbalances occur because significant differences in vocabulary and test-taking techniques have developed over time and are correlated with race and socioeconomic status.

■ Traditional Tests and Racism

Perhaps one of the best illustrations of this issue is provided by an examination of the intelligence scores of Italian Americans over the past three generations. When a substantial number of Italian-Americans were new to the United States and had limited language facility, limited opportunities for education, and limited social recognition, their exam scores were the lowest among European ethnic groups. This, of course, conformed with the prejudices of the intelligence test bureaucrats of the 1920s, who were convinced that southern and eastern Europeans were genetically inferior to northern Europeans. It was no coincidence that the historical record reflects that these men were also active in the eugenics movement—a popular academic and political movement to "purify" the gene pool in America.

The test administrators and race purists didn't count on one thing—Italian-Americans, as any other ethnic group, would eventually learn the game. Over time and through succeeding generations, Italian-Americans achieved scores that steadily increased to the point that they are now higher than the other average European-American scores and even higher than the average American scores.[3] Thus the use of norms did not provide a meaningful distinction for Italian-Americans any more than it does today for any other ethnic groups whose test scores are compared to others. Such a competitive system provides a false sense of achievement to sluggards who score in the upper third, but who still don't know their multiplication tables. If the evidence of many international math and science student performance tests have demonstrated anything, it is that we should take little comfort from being "above average" in a country whose eighth grade students consistently rank far behind their counterparts in other nations. Finally, competition gives a false sense of inability to those in the lower third who have never been taught their multiplication tables.

---

3.   Perkins, D.N. (1995). *Outsmarting IQ: The emerging science of learnable intelligence.* New York: The Free Press.

■ Standards Promote Mixed Ability Grouping. Norms Promote Segregation of Students by Ability.

Many modern teachers sneer at the "blackbirds and bluebirds" reading groups of twenty-five years ago and recall the insidious impact such a labeling dichotomy had upon children. Regardless, strong and vocal constituencies remain who support the concept, if not the names, of ability groups. The evidence, however, is strikingly in favor of mixed ability student groups. Not only does the performance of less able students improve when they are matched with students who can serve as peer coaches, but the performance of the coaches themselves improves. With mixed ability groups these coaches are in a position to articulate their knowledge, help another person, and think through the cognitive steps of a solution. Without the challenge of mixed ability grouping, this variety of ideas might not have occurred to them. This conforms to common experience—one tends to master a subject better when one is forced to teach it, rather than study it.

■ Standards Are Challenging. Norms Provide Excuses for a "Dumbed Down" Curriculum.

One of the more extraordinary political charges made against the standards movement is that it lowers educational expectations. In fact, precisely the contrary is true. A norm-based concept of achievement allows a student who is proficient in arithmetic and has a rudimentary acquaintance with algebra, to score very well on standardized high school mathematics tests. Yet such a student would not come close to meeting the standards-based high school graduation requirements many districts have adopted. Those requirements include a demonstration of proficiency in algebra, geometry, trigonometry, statistics, and, in some cases, even calculus. Although it is a rare district, indeed, that has been able to turn out graduates who universally achieve these requirements, the enforcement of high school graduation requirements is the only mechanism by which such challenging and rigorous standards will ever become part of the universal curriculum.

As long as districts rely upon norms, mathematically illiterate students with above-average preparation in a suburban district will generally score better on standardized tests than students in urban districts. Because the urban districts are more numerous, suburban districts will be secure in their "above average" label while performing at a mediocre level. This is even more apparent in grade school, where the differentiation among the latter elementary grades is striking, with some students barely able to read and others mastering many number operations. The fifth grade student who is merely a proficient reader and able to perform rudimentary addition, subtraction, multiplication, and division, is given a false sense of security by scoring in the upper twenty-five percent of norm-based tests. Yet such a student may not achieve even half the fifth grade academic standards that a standards-based system of achievement would require.

▓ Standards Are Complicated. Norms Are Simple.

A generation of psychometricians has thrived on the complexity that norm-referenced tests and its sequelae have engendered. (I am indebted to Robert LeMahieu for the appellation "recovering psychometrician," a label I gladly accept.) Despite the superficial complexity of manipulations of statistical distributions, norm-referenced tests offer the public the artificial simplicity of reducing student performance to a single number. "Your child is a 136," say the norm-referenced advocates with satisfaction, though they have not a clue as to the level of proficiency such a number represents. What they know for sure, however, is that there were very few who scored a 136, which means that a 136 is good. Such labels are comparable to a doctor calling the patient into her office and announcing, "I have good news and bad news—your x-factor is 136, but your y-factor is an 88. Have a nice day." Such a cryptic message from a doctor would be regarded as malpractice. The same misuse of meaningless numbers, accompanied by little or no explanation and carrying implications of grave weight and predictive power, is in the nature of educational malpractice when done by school districts, test vendors, and teachers.

▓ Using Test Scores to Improve Teaching and Learning

The other extreme—keeping test scores secret because "parents wouldn't understand them anyway"—is equally destructive. What is required is a test data reporting system that clearly shows parents, teachers, students, and educational leaders two things: do the students meet the standard, and what areas need the most focus in planning next year's curriculum? Incredibly, for the millions of dollars spent on testing in the U.S., these two fundamental questions are rarely answered. Scores are almost invariably reported against a norm or average. On many occasions I have asked the basic question, "How many problems did the student get right and how many did he get wrong?" Only rarely have test directors or national test companies been able to provide an answer—"we're not programmed to do that," they explain. If teachers and leaders cannot analyze individual test items, they cannot plan their classes to improve student performance. Frequently, the only "analysis" comes down to bromides such as "math scores are down—let's do more math!"

The Board of Education, amidst some disgust about kids these days not knowing math the way their grandparents did, votes to increase the number of hours spent in math. But rarely is a strategic analysis of curriculum, learning, assessment, and time undertaken. A standards-based approach would begin and end with one question—what must students know and be able to do? Then curriculum, assessment, and time requirements would be based on the answer to that question—an answer, by the way, that might be different for different students. Classes and times might change, but learning expectations would remain uniform for all students. Finally, a standards-based approach to test data would include many different assessments and not make curriculum and other strategic decisions based on a single indicator taken on a single spring afternoon.

■ Standards Address Causes, Intermediate Effects, and Achievement. Norms Reflect Only Test Scores.

The second generation of standards will address not only academic content, but also the antecedents to academic achievement. My colleagues at the Center for Performance Assessment[SM] have developed a family support scale (see Figure 9.3, page 80), which conveys to parents the importance of their role in the academic achievement of students. Although a breakdown of student mathematical and reading achievement is important, a family support scale that identifies antecedents to achievement of academic standards is even more crucial. Examples include the following:

- I read with my child 15 minutes every day.

- I limit television to not more than two hours every evening.

- I review my child's homework every day.

- I have at least one meal per day with my child, and during this time the television is turned off.

No doubt readers can think of many more. Other creative schools have included standards describing participation in extracurricular activities, development of artistic and musical appreciation, participation in community service projects, and levels of parental involvement. Every one of these antecedents represents not only measurable and standards-based achievements, but also is all demonstrably linked to academic achievement.

Because the causes of academic achievement are varied and complex, a meaningful reporting system must consider not only the ultimate effects, but also the causes and intermediate effects. Such a system helps to provide important early warnings signals where performance appears to be inadequate.

■ The Impulse Toward Ranking

Even in a district without norms, ranks, or comparisons, there will remain the inevitable impulse toward competition. Frequently, this is fueled by the academic equivalent of the "little league dad" who must live out his fantasies of academic victories through his children. It is never enough for the demanding "little league dad" that his son—almost always a son—is playing ball, having a good time, and enjoying the game. He must successfully hit every ball, catch every throw, run every base, and accomplish every unfulfilled dream of the frustrated father.

The desire to go beyond satisfaction to competition is not part of the human spirit, but part of modern day psychosis. One can hardly imagine the "little league dad's" prehistoric ancestor, having had his fill of reptile flesh, immediately becoming dissatisfied when noticing more bones beside his neighbor's campfire. When satisfying hunger was a standard, enough was enough. Meeting the standard was all that counted—eating more than one's neighbor was not required. Somewhere along the line, however, sufficiency gave way to superiority, and this disease still affects us today. Newspapers love to rank schools. One member of the education research community recently remarked that if we treated psychological tests the same way that we treat educational tests, *USA Today* would be the first to publish the nation's top ten neurotic states, the top ten egomaniac cities, and the best counties for depression. I am not suggesting that sufficiency is an alternative to knowledge for its own sake. I am suggesting that sufficiency is an alternative to the meaningless competition in classrooms and the idea of "beating the other person" for the sake of victory without substance.

■ Making the Case for Standards to a Skeptical Public

Successful transformation from norms to standards requires an iron political will—the sort of will that can withstand the abuse of critics who will claim that the failure to publish norms, or even to discover how a district is performing compared to norms, represents hiding from bad news. It requires the will to demonstrate to those critics that, were they were infected with a dread disease, their objective to become cured would be paramount. And if such a cure were to arrive, they would not become dissatisfied if their white cell count showed them to be somewhat less "cured" than a neighbor who had a similar disease. Rather, their only hope would be to be healthy, fully recovered, and cured. Making these arguments requires patience, repetition, and seemingly interminable explanations. Ironically, this is the same effort we expect from the average elementary teacher and that seems appropriate for the average student in the primary grades. We must be at least as willing to pursue such laborious strategies with critics who cannot, or will not, understand the importance of the movement toward standards.

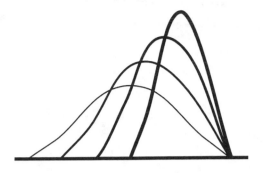

chapter four

Standards-Based Assessments—The Key to Standards Implementation

More than forty-five states have either implemented academic content standards or are in the process of developing them. The documents associated with these standards outline a set of expectations for the knowledge, performance, and achievement by students in the public schools of those states. Unfortunately, however, the link between the promise of standards and the reality of their implementation is a tenuous one. States that adopt new standards, but retain old assessments, should not be surprised that the test content will drive educational practice. Unless standards are linked to assessments, the standards become little more than a political slogan full of good, but empty, intentions.

In Chapter 3, we outlined the reasons standards are different from norms. These differences are important not just in theory, but in the day-to-day practice of the classroom teacher. It is in accountability and assessment where the most dramatic differences are evident between a standards-based approach and a traditional approach to education. Standards are not simply a different method of labeling traditional curriculum contents, but are fundamentally different. In this chapter we will contrast these differences.

■ The Traditional Assessment

1. The assessment is secret.

Consider for a moment the principles that underlie traditional assessment. The assessment is a secret. The contents of the tests are typically locked away and revealed only at the moment when students break the seal on the test booklet. Teachers and principals who fail to maintain the test security lose their jobs. Teachers who teach the test are regarded as unethical.

The traditional test uses advanced statistical programs to look for patterns of student responses in which a large number of students respond to questions in the same way. This would indicate that the question was not ideal. One might express surprise at this expectation—after all, students who have been in a classroom for 180 days with the same teacher receiving the same instruction might be expected to answer the same questions in the same way. This logic, however, does not penetrate the veil of mysticism that surrounds traditional testing. Students are victims of the immutable bell curve and no amount of instruction will change the normal distribution of their answers. Any deviation from this is to be regarded with suspicion.

2. Traditional tests are associated with national norms.

Chapter 3 addressed some of the important differences between standards and norms. For the moment, however, it is important to note that norms-based assessments are predicated on the notion that the objective of every classroom teacher is to "beat" teachers in other parts of the country who are part of the normed study.

This impulse to be above average is fostered by the test companies themselves, who are able to report data in such a way that nearly every district and state in the nation can claim to be above average, something most students know is an impossibility. Worse yet, the impulse to be above average takes precedence over the demand for knowledge. There are functionally illiterate students who can answer a sufficient quantity of multiple choice questions to be in the middle band of national tests results. It should be worrisome that professional educators, not to mention parents and policy makers, could be satisfied with such an inadequate level of performance. Nonetheless, the traditional approach to assessment takes comfort not in achievement, but in the average.

3. Traditional assessments seek to discriminate among different students.

The ideal test item is one that a substantial number of students will get wrong. These are regarded in the test industry as good discriminators, not because they discriminate in a sense of racial or cultural bias, but because they distinguish one student from another. A test item that through the hard work of students and teachers is answered correctly by every single student is regarded as a poor discriminator. If a test item fails to differentiate among students, it serves no statistical purpose. Of course, the practical result of this process is to systematically discourage both students and teachers—something inconsequential to the traditional assessment advocates.

4. Traditional assessments are overwhelmingly multiple choice tests.

The selection of the multiple choice method of testing is the result of two factors. First, when tests are given in large numbers they must be graded by computers and only multiple choice tests readily submit to computer grading. Second, there is a certain statistical neatness to multiple choice responses—some answers are clearly wrong and other answers are clearly right. The fact that our complex world rarely offers such neat distinctions is another factor that is lost on the advocates of traditional assessment.

5. Traditional assessments are typically limited in time.

Most students are conditioned to expect one week of terror in the spring, when classroom instruction comes to a halt and testing begins. During that week, children are admonished to eat good breakfasts, get plenty of sleep, and pay attention. Class schedules are rigorous, the hallways are silent, and extra attention is paid to every detail. The level of anxiety and tension is palpable. Students and teachers know there is something very different about testing, and it is not at all the same as regular education.

■ Why Standards-Based Assessments Are Important

There are some districts and states that have implemented standards but still maintain the "week of test terror" approach to assessment. Such a change is illusory with little impact on daily instruction and classroom practice. It is as if traditional assessments were the "emperor who wore new clothes," and after many meetings of advisors, the problem of the emperor's apparent nudity is solved by having him wear an expensive, ostentatious tie. The fundamental result is the same, but those engaged in the energy and expense to adorn the emperor with a new tie failed to realize that they have not engendered a fundamental change.

Standards are closely linked with expectations and a large body of evidence suggests that high expectations lead to better student achievement. It is also reasonable to say that expectations alone do not generate fundamental change. Standards without standards-based assessments are merely a very expensive and time-consuming pep talk—one in a string of educational initiatives and innovations that shed more heat than light.

■ Why Standards-Based Assessments Are Different

1. Standards-based assessments are open, not secret.

One innovative program is in the Milwaukee Public Schools, where standards-based assessments have been in use for two years with remarkable improvements in student performance. In the Milwaukee program, teachers are given as many as sixteen standards-based assessments at the beginning of the year. One of these will be used for the spring-time assessment. Teachers are encouraged to use the assessments not just as "a practice test" but as part of their daily teaching activities. Students write, read, solve mathematical problems, and generally do things in class that they and their teachers know will be directly related to what they will be doing on the test.

This may seem to be nothing more than common sense and clear logic, but it is dramatically different from the veil of secrecy that shrouds traditional assessments. In the classrooms in which standards-based assessments have become fully integrated, assessments happen frequently, not as a terror-filled week, but as part of daily classroom activities. The contents of the assessments are not secret, but are known by and discussed among the students. Rather than being locked in a safe, assessments are freely distributed to students, parents, and teachers, so that the expectations about performance are clearly understood by all constituents.

2. Standards-based assessments are designed so that a large number of students—ideally every student—can achieve proficiency.

When a large number of students fail to succeed at a particular challenge on a standards-based assessment, that item is not regarded as "a good discriminator." Rather, it is a signal that more work needs to be done in the classroom. Standards-based classrooms are built on a philosophical foundation that every child can learn, rather than the philosophy that every child has a fixed place on the bell curve from which movement is unlikely to occur.

3. Standards-based assessments involve a demonstration of proficiency, not a guess on a multiple choice test.

When discussing this subject before workshops and other audiences, I will usually issue the challenge, "Will everyone who has never guessed on a multiple choice test please stand up and holler." In hundreds of workshops and speeches across the country, I have never once had a participant holler or otherwise give any other indication that they have failed to guess. This is an important point because critics of standards-based performance assessments believe that multiple choice tests are inherently more rigorous and objective than standards-based performance assessments. On the contrary, when a student has a choice of A, B, C, or D as a response, there is a 25 percent chance that they can guess correctly, thereby "demonstrating" proficiency on that test item when they are clearly not proficient.

In a performance assessment, by contrast, students are able to demonstrate proficiency when they genuinely have mastered the subject. This criterion would apply to problems in science, mathematics, social studies, and English. It is impossible to assess student writing with any degree of confidence by having the students take a multiple choice test about grammar and punctuation. On the contrary, it is indispensable to assess student writing by having them write a passage designed to describe or persuade.

It is evident that the logistics of performance assessments are much more complex than running thousands of answers sheets through an electronic scanner. The supposed need for the efficiency of electronic answer sheets is based on the premise that assessments occur only during one week, and hence thousands of tests must be graded in a very short period of time. In a classroom in which standards-based performance assessments predominate, however, there is no such thing as the week of terror associated with traditional tests. Rather, assessments happen every week of the year. Teachers collaborate on grading, revising, and creating new assessments. When large-scale assessments are conducted by a school district or state, teachers participate in evaluating the student work so that they can have a clear idea of what other students in the same grade are able to accomplish. This becomes an important professional development activity for the teacher rather than a mindless administrative task in which bubbles on an answer sheet are compared to letters in a scoring guide.

4. Performance assessments recognize the fact that there is not a single "right" answer on a number of test items.

Consider two examples, one for first grade and one for college students attempting to enter graduate school. Both make the point that a computer—or for that matter, a teacher, administrator, or board member—that recognizes only one "right" answer would be failing to recognize student achievement. The examples in Figure 4.1 are not contrived, but are taken from tests that have been administered within the last twelve months.

figure 4.1
Only One "Right" Answer

Elementary Example

In this first example, the first grade student was given the following story problem:

Mary had four balls. John had three balls.
How many balls did they have all together? (Show your work.)

In the traditional method of assessment, the only "right" response was the following:

4 + 3 = 7

One enterprising student, however, took the directions quite literally and responded as follows:

Using a traditional assessment method, the student who answered in the first manner received a satisfactory score, while the student who responded in second manner received a failing score. Clearly both students understood the directions and responded appropriately.

College Example

This second example is a test of vocabulary and analytical reasoning ability by college students who hoped to gain entrance into graduate school.

Identify the relationship between the words hatch and hold.

For the student who grew up going to summer camp on the east coast and learned her way around a sloop, these were obvious references to different parts of a boat. To the land-locked student, who had a vocabulary and analytical reasoning skills equal to his counterpart on the east coast, the relationship between the two words had to do with procedures in chicken breeding. Only standards-based performance assessments—those that allow the evaluator to consider whether or not the student demonstrated proficiency in the subject at hand—would properly give credit to both of these responses.

5. Standards-based performance assessments force educators to come to grips with this central question: "What do we expect of our students?"

If the answer to that question is, "We expect them to color in an oval with a number two pencil in a box that corresponds to the expectations of a test item writer, who may or may not have the slightest clue about the requirements of our curriculum in the conduct of our classes," then traditional assessments will fit the bill nicely. If, on the other hand, the response to this central question is, "We expect students to demonstrate proficiency in the standards that our community, our school district, and our state have established," then only standards-based performance assessments will suffice.

■ Self-Esteem and Assessment

Much ridicule has been directed toward assessment practices that substitute self-esteem for academic rigor. This criticism is appropriate in many cases where students have been permitted to demonstrate unsatisfactory performance and still receive rewards and recognition from teachers and schools. There is, indeed, a cult of self-esteem which holds that giving "bad news" about school performance can produce undue damage to children. Therefore, self-esteem of the child is elevated above the truth. Unfortunately, the response to this sort of nonsense has frequently been equally nonsensical. There are undeniably silly things that have been done in classrooms in the name of self-esteem, but the cure for this silliness is not a retreat to Neanderthal assessment techniques.

Most adults can recognize at least some moments in their lives when they actually enjoyed learning something. Typically, this was associated with their ability to demonstrate performance in something at which they were particularly good, and for which they received a certain amount of external praise and internal satisfaction. Moreover, when it was their time to "perform," they knew precisely what was expected of them. Standards-based performance assessments follow that model and, as a result, students are able to approach the last week of April not with a sense of dread at the impending test week, but rather with a sense of confidence. Ideally, students should be able to open the book of assessments and say confidently to themselves, "been there, done that," and then proceed with the assessment. Properly prepared students see nothing new in the spring assessments. They should see only a slightly different form of the assessments they have been completing every week since school began. Assessment is not a "gotcha!" In the words of one of the nation's leading performance assessment researchers, Dr. Lorrie Shepherd, assessments should be an opportunity for students to "show what they know."

The principal objective of this book is to facilitate the implementation of academic content standards by using standards-based performance assessments in the classroom and home. There is no longer a wall that divides teaching and testing, but rather assessment will become an integral part of the teaching process. Instead of being locked away in safes, tests are scattered about classrooms, lunchrooms, and coffee tables. Instead of being a subject reserved for discussion among the priesthood of psychometricians, assessments are freely discussed by students, teachers, and parents. Most importantly, everyone involved in the educational process has confidence that assessments directly reflect the standards which the school, community, and state have established. People who know what the standards are will also know what the assessments will contain. Rather than regarding "teaching the test" as an unethical educational practice, teaching within the framework of standards is, by definition, the only sort of teaching that takes place and is directly linked to the standards-based performance assessments that students receive throughout the year.

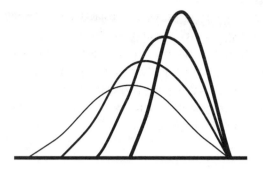

chapter five

Standards-Based Assessments—How Are They Better?

Consider this hypothetical situation:

> You have just returned from a conference where you were exposed to some exciting new ideas in your field. You are anxious to share this information with your colleagues, not only because it is good for your organization, but because you genuinely believe in what you have heard. This may not be a magic bullet, but you believe these ideas will help your company, department, or school. At a meeting of your colleagues, there is not only a remarkable lack of enthusiasm, but the cynicism is palpable. Finally, it is voiced: "We've heard it all before." While a few others chuckle, another chimes in: "This, too, shall pass."

Your enthusiasm crushed, you return home wondering if innovation ever has a chance in this place.

Being enthusiastic is not enough. Ideas competing for the attention of busy teachers, administrators, and policy makers must have merit not only in theory, but in practice. The simple question, "What is the bottom line?" must be addressed before we can expect educators or anyone else to implement standards and performance assessments. It is not sufficient to simply answer, "It is the law."

Bureaucracies, including educational ones, are notorious for being resistant to change regardless of the mandates surrounding them. Educators are, after all, part of the discipline that developed motivation theory. Therefore, it should not be surprising to them that extrinsic motivators such as carrots and sticks are far less effective than intrinsic motivational forces associated with improving the worth of teachers as professionals and as people. Thus, in an appeal to this most noble and most effective form of motivation, we consider the issue of why standards-based performance assessments are better. Why, after all, is it worth the inconvenience to change the way we have been teaching?

There are four fundamental answers to this question. The answers include fairness, specificity, process-orientation, and relevance. These four powerful characteristics are the prime differentiators between traditional assessments and standards-based performance assessments.

■ Fairness

Imagine you were asked to play a game with a group of people. Unfortunately, none of them speak your language. Nevertheless, they insist that you join the game. You notice that the area in which you are playing is bounded by red lines and there are baskets at each end of this area. Then you are handed a ball. This group communicates with you by their expressions and voices. From this communication you deduce that you are a member of the red team and proceed to take the ball and place it in one of the two baskets.

The people on the blue team scream with delight, while your team-mates look at you in disgust. You notice that the score board displays the number one for the blue team. Again, you have the ball, and this time, learning from your mistake, you place the ball in the other basket. Wrong guess—the blue team is ecstatic, and the score is now two to zero.

Next, one of the blue team members comes up to you and, as he takes the ball away from you, knocks you to the ground with a blow that leaves you seeing stars. Before you can get up, you notice that the opposing blue team was awarded another point, apparently for knocking you down. Three to zero. Your team-mates are now screaming at you, apparently encouraging you to get back on your feet and get back in the game.

You go over to the player who had so unceremoniously knocked you down a moment ago, and return the favor by taking the ball and dispatching him with an elbow to the solar plexus. Now you are sent to the penalty box and the blue team is awarded ten points. Though you cannot understand their language, you discern that your team-mates have decided that you are irredeemably stupid and utterly unable to play their game. How do you feel?

If you absorb the physical and emotional imagery of this scene, you might have an inkling of what a child feels when she has brought home reams of papers with smiling faces and high marks, and then takes a test that makes her feel incompetent. You might feel like the student who has graduated from high school with a "C" average and finds out that he cannot get a job at the factory because he cannot complete the application forms and initial testing battery for new employees. You might feel like the student whose cooperative manner has earned him a "B" average in his classes in one school, but after transferring to a cross-town high school, finds that he is two years behind and is failing every course. You would feel cheated, betrayed, useless, and sick.

These games all have one thing in common: their primary obligation is not to be fair, but rather to systematically report that there were winners and losers. All of these games perform the function of dividing the participants into two groups: winners and losers.

- **What Does "Fairness" in Testing Mean?**

   For a test to be fair it must, above all, conform to the common principle that every child on every playground knows: You must know the rules before you can be expected to play the game. Yet every year in thousands of school districts, millions of children are subjected to the academic equivalent of the mystery game described above. School districts think that they are assessing these students when, in fact, they are learning little about the students' academic achievement. These tests, secretive by nature, are based on general content fields, but are not specifically linked to the curriculum, textbooks, or teaching practices in that district. Therefore, the "winners" on these tests do not demonstrate effective educational strategies, but effective guessing and test-taking techniques.

- **Standards-Based Tests Are Different**

   When standards are a public document, making clear to every parent, teacher, and student what is expected, there is a community consensus about what makes one proficient. Then the community develops a commitment to the principle that all students can achieve the standards, though there is an acknowledgment that some students will need more time, assistance, and resources to become proficient. Some students will need more help learning the language. Others will need assistance in basic skills, which their previous school did not provide. Still others may need enough food to allow them to concentrate on their lessons. But all students can eventually meet the standards. Because every student knows what is expected and precisely what the standards are, no student is ever asked to play a game in which the rules are a secret. No child becomes a "loser" because she guesses wrong. No child is limited to a "one-shot" opportunity to become a "winner." And most importantly, becoming a "winner" does not depend on an equal number of your classmates becoming "losers." Because of the openness of the process and the public ownership of the standards, fairness is inherent in standards-based assessments.

■ Specificity

The national love affair with "the basics" has a certain appeal. We like to reduce things to their simple elements, such as readin', writin', and 'rithmetic (the three R's). But as Albert Einstein wisely said, "Things should be made as simple as possible, but not more so."

In fact, these three R's do not tell students and parents very much at all about what is expected, while content standards provide a high degree of specificity. Students will know, for example, that fractions and decimals are important for fourth graders, but trigonometry is not. They will know that by high school, they will be expected to understand trigonometric properties of plane and solid figures, but the understanding they acquire in the earlier grades will lead directly to higher levels of mathematical understanding. They will also know that math alone is insufficient for their success. They must also be able to effectively communicate their mathematical knowledge in written and oral presentations. The tests these students take in high school are not a mysterious "gotcha!" but an open and public set of expectations for which students have spent years preparing.

■ Process-Orientation

While traditional tests focus on the product—typically the answers to a set of test questions— the standards-based performance tests focus on the process. A student is not a "failure" if, during his first attempt to solve a problem, he writes a wrong answer. Rather, an important part of the assessment process is the revision and continuous improvement of the student's work product. Research demonstrates conclusively that one of the most powerful tools teachers can use to improve student writing is (no surprise) editing and rewriting. Tests that allow students to turn in only one draft of a paper (such as many of the essay tests now used in high schools and colleges) fly in the face of this research. Such tests encourage the "Saturday night special" mentality, in which students give any assignment their "best shot" and then move to the next project.

Performance assessments, by contrast, encourage students to try, revise, improve, and try again. This is the process by which most scientific advancement has been achieved. We hope this process will be ingrained into those who build bridges, fly airplanes, and mend bodies. The most effective workers, from the factory floor to the executive suite, are those who systematically and consistently observe, modify, and improve their performance. Standards-based performance assessments allow students to start this process at a much earlier age.

■ Process and Accuracy—A Critical Combination

Critics of performance assessment have been quick to ridicule assessments in which process is emphasized because they argue that any consideration of process must de-emphasize the need for accuracy. This is an important argument and it deserves a complete answer. First, there is no dichotomy between accuracy and process—both are essential for a student to demonstrate proficiency. In writing, students must not only have the ability to demonstrate the process of creating an informative essay, but they must also spell and punctuate their essay correctly. In mathematics, students must not only solve the problem in a logical sequence using appropriate processes, but they must also solve it accurately. Any good performance assessment requires both process and accuracy—not one or the other.

Second, if there is a danger of improper emphasis associated with a test format, it is the danger that multiple choice tests pose when they allow students and teachers to assume proficiency when the right letter is selected, while the student does not understand how the answer was achieved.

Third, our technical, professional, and leadership jobs of the future require the ability to communicate about solutions to problems. That is why the most effective math and science standards, for example, require students to communicate about the application of mathematical and scientific principles to real world problems. Calculation ability alone, or communication ability alone, are insufficient—the challenges of a technological world require students who have mastered process, accuracy, and communication about the problems they are attempting to solve.

■ Relevance

The tests that many students take are mind-numbingly boring and strikingly irrelevant to the worlds of work and life. It is not uncommon for employers to express shock that students are completely unfamiliar with the world of work. This is largely a reflection of the fact that so little of the language and activity of the work place has been included in school life.

Standards-based performance assessments can change this. They can provide extended assignments, challenging students to engage in real world activities. Students in science classes do not answer questions about the chemical composition of a compound using pencil and paper. They conduct an experiment and analyze the compound. Students in an English class do not take a vocabulary test. They write an essay demonstrating that they can effectively communicate using the vocabulary words they have learned. Students in a geometry class do not write down page after page of equations involving angles and sides. They design a building showing the application of their skills.

The outcome is not just greater student interest, though that surely would be sufficient to justify a move toward standards-based performance assessments. Of equal importance is the outcome of rebuilding the bridge between the business community and public education. This relationship has been almost destroyed in the past three decades as educators have regarded vocational endeavors as the polar opposite of education. As a result, business people have allowed their discontent with the products of the educational system to lead them to feelings of unrestrained contempt.

Performance assessments offer both educators and business people the opportunity to stop posturing and to identify the many areas they have in common. Teachers want to make their tests more relevant and interesting. Business people want students to emerge from school acquainted with work place expectations. Together, both parties can help to make that happen. The articulation of standards (and their associated performance assessments) are an excellent foundation upon which those conversations can focus.

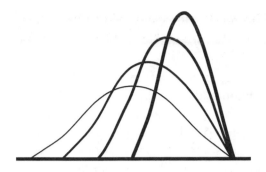

chapter six

The Role of the Classroom Teacher

Not long ago, I sat at a table with a number of the nation's leading experts on public school standards. After one person spoke at length about the need for staff development in order to implement standards, the moderator, an official from the U.S. Department of Education with many years of experience in both the government and the classroom said, "If we have learned anything in the course of several decades of educational reform, it is that attempting to change behavior through staff development does not work."

Although I devote more than two hundred days each year to teacher and administrator seminars, I must confess that this statement is true—staff development does not lead to educational reform. Staff development efforts in districts throughout the nation have consumed an extraordinary amount of resources, having a minuscule impact on teaching and learning in the classroom. This is particularly true of the all too typical staff development model, which is best described as a "dog and pony show" or, more recently, the "sage on the stage." In this model, an "expert"—always from a distant city—comes in and "shares" some mechanism of teaching, analysis, assessment, or other more chic term of educational nomenclature. The presentations are invariably regarded as new and exclusive, known only to the cognoscenti, and the suggestion that any of these emperors might be wearing no clothes would be to brand oneself as not being sufficiently innovative or reform-minded.

Most readers of this book have probably witnessed many such presentations and would concur, with perhaps a few notable exceptions. These "expert" presentations range from a blinding flash of the obvious to the patently absurd, with notions concocted by people who have not set foot in a real classroom with real children in many years, if ever. The research on recent educational innovations by Ellis and Fouts (see footnote, page 26) has effectively stripped some of these methods of the claim to be "research-based."

It is essential to note at the outset that, although the term staff development may be associated with standards implementation, the traditional "dog and pony show" model will not work. A substantial body of research suggests that, in the area of standards-based assessments, consistency by teachers is not achieved until they have actively participated in at least twenty hours of hands-on workshops. This is consistent with my own experience. In a five day standards-based assessment workshop, Monday and Tuesday are typically a mixture of chaos and resentment, with comments ranging from "This too shall pass—one more reform effort that won't be here a year from now," to "Why are we doing this? You mean to tell me that what we have been doing for the last twenty years has been wrong?" Amidst this frustration, resentment, and cynicism, all of a facilitator's efforts are expended in maintaining a semblance of organization.

But there is a point—typically about Wednesday afternoon—when a significant break-through occurs. This is not a gradual process, but a threshold. The laborious process of associating content standards with individual tasks occurs more rapidly as participants become more familiar with standards. Consensus on the type of work that constitutes achievement of standards or progress towards standards is achieved more quickly. Scoring guides are worded more precisely and with greater clarity, with less dissent among the group.[4] The difference between Wednesday morning and Wednesday afternoon is astonishing. Inter-rater reliability jumps from 20-30 percent all the way to 70-80 percent.[5] Cynicism, while not completely absent, is the exception rather than the rule. Suggestions are made for innovative applications, and extraordinary things start to occur. Most importantly, there is a feeling among the participants that, with this level of initial mastery in standards-based teaching, the whole concept not only has merit, but just might work. This will never happen as the result of an inspirational speech or a school directive. It will happen only with a commitment to many hours in professional reorientation at the classroom level. At the end of this chapter (Figures 6.1-6.2, pages 52-55) is an example of a staff development curriculum provided by the Center for Performance Assessment, that districts may wish to consider.

Of course, for standards to make the jump from the blackboard during a staff development workshop to actual classroom practice, more than mere training sessions are required. The application of standards requires a commitment on the part of teachers to engage in specific classroom activities relating directly to standards. If this is going to happen, it is necessary to pull the weeds before planting the flowers. (More about pulling weeds is covered in Chapter 13.) Where are the weeds? They are all around us. Classroom practice is typically full of activities bearing little or no relationship to the district's academic standards. To the extent

---

4.   Scoring guides are the documents used to determine whether the work is exemplary, proficient, progressing toward the standard, or not yet meeting the standard. A Standards Achievement Report (SAR) is an example of one such guide. These topics are covered in more detail in Chapters 9 and 17.

5.   Inter-rater reliability is a term used to describe the relationship of the scores (ratings) among two or more judges (raters). It can be computed in a variety of ways from simple correlations to percentage of agreement. Here the larger numbers indicate a greater degree of agreement.

that there is a link, it is more likely to be made by the publishers of workbooks or textbooks than by principals and teachers.

Student work is typically broken into discreet assignments—the "drill and kill" method—more remarkable for their quantity than quality. I cannot count the number of times I have heard teachers state, with more than a hint of resentment at even discussing the subject, that they are "of course teaching in a standards-based manner, of course teaching problem-solving techniques, and of course teaching higher level thinking skills." I then ask these teachers for a typical parent packet that contains a week of one student's papers. The packet is often full, and provides the pleasant illusion for both teacher and parent that a great deal of activity and learning is taking place. But an examination of the contents of the packet reveals otherwise. Page after page is devoted to repetitious skills that require thinking at the lowest level. Even more astonishing (and environmentally offensive) is the number of instances the paper is largely comprised of workbook directions, with only a sentence fragment or two of student expression contained on each page. The requirement to cover the subject matter leaves teachers claiming they have little choice, and their commitment to completing the workbook is one designed more to demonstrate comprehensiveness than comprehension.

■ Pull the Weeds and Prepare the Soil.

Before standards can be effectively implemented in the classroom, the teacher must review every assignment and classroom activity. The simple question is, "To what standard does this activity relate?" If it does not appear to relate to an academic content standard, then one of two things is true. Either there is a grave omission in the academic standards that should be corrected, or the activity should be discontinued.

Some of these activities are directly under the control of the teacher. There are teachers who have devoted many hours to activities such as insect collections, or acting out the last days of the Alamo. The activities include student government, dramatic productions, and so on—all of which can be excellent standards-based activities when they are linked to standards—but some may not have had the slightest link to academic content standards. In other cases, the activities themselves may have promise, but are unrelated to the achievement level for that particular grade. This is particularly true in elementary school mathematics, where far too many fifth graders are continuing to complete worksheets on a level at which the teacher is comfortable, but the students are not proceeding to learn disciplines such as ratios, decimals, fractions, and critical pre-algebra skills that will prepare them for secondary school mathematics. Pulling the weeds is a difficult process, not unlike cleaning out an old closet or emptying a desk containing years of mementos. It can even be painful, but it is necessary. Standards cannot be effectively implemented in a classroom that clings to pre-standards activities.

■ Identify the Standards-Based Assessments that Will Be Used for Accountability Purposes.

Unfortunately, some districts have failed to articulate these standards, or worse yet, they claim to be standards-based, but continue to keep the assessment activities a secret. Their words contain the vocabulary of standards, but their policies and educational actions betray a commitment to the old norm-referenced regime. If your district has not made standards-based assessment explicitly available, then the teacher can nevertheless find clones of standards-based assignments, including those in Part Four of this book.

■ Identify the "Best Practices" in Standards-Based Teaching and Learning in Your Area.

This means not only attending a workshop, but rather spending time listening to and learning from other teachers who have developed their own standards-based classroom activities. Identify one academic area for development of your own standards-based activities. Remember as a first year teacher how difficult it was to develop lesson plans for every subject simultaneously? It was exhausting, and some of the lesson plans were not as good as you would have liked them to be. The good news is that standards implementation does not have to be on such a rushed basis. There are so many assignments available that it is possible to rely on those that have been provided by others. An essential goal of standards-based teaching and learning is that the teacher develops his or her own standards-based assignments and assessments. A reasonable goal is that over the course of four years, teachers might be able to cover the curriculum for which they are responsible. But for the first year, pick just one area, and develop your own activities in that particular area.

■ Have Students Put Standards and Scoring Guides in their Own Words.

All too frequently, the language of standards and scoring guides is a professional one, designed to allow one educator to speak to another. It is much more important that these standards come alive for our students. One of my favorite examples appeared on a bulletin board in a first grade classroom in a small rural community of a western state. This teacher, among the most professional standards-based teachers I have witnessed, asked her students to put the standards into their own words. The students had, accordingly, identified what they needed to do to get a rating of 4, 3, 2 or 1 representing exemplary, proficient, progressing toward the standard, or not meeting the standard. On the board was the note "I get a 2 if I squish my letters like a fuzzy worm." I have yet to meet a psychometrician who was able to write with such precision.

■ Conduct Weekly Reflective Evaluations of Your Classroom Practice.

Whenever a major change is taking place in one's professional or personal life, the activity of writing one's reactions, reflections, and observations is invaluable. Too often educational evaluation has focused only on test scores. An essential part of the standards movement is that our concept of effectiveness and our framework for evaluation extends far beyond test scores alone, and includes levels of student engagement in the process, levels of teacher passion for the process, and levels of innovation through the process. Journaling is an excellent means of conducting such an introspective evaluation.

■ Identify a Small Group With Whom Your Successes and Challenges Can Be Shared.

A faculty meeting is rarely the forum for this. Rather, schools should provide opportunities for teachers who are committed to standards and who share a common professional interest to meet on a regular basis. A group of four to six is ideal—fewer than that does not provide for sustainability, while greater than that number can tend to become overly bureaucratic, with too much listening and not enough sharing.

■ Share Your Successes With Others.

The foundation of effective implementation of standards is the periodic publication of best practices by schools and districts. Effective teachers are willing to contribute to this process. There is no question that there are a variety of impediments to the implementation of standards or to any educational reform. But the ones I hear most frequently are lack of support, lack of resources, lack of parental involvement, and so on. But the proverbial bottom line is this: no amount of policies, workshops, and consultants is worth the effort or resources if they are expended on things that do not change classroom practices or do not implement standards at the classroom level.

figure 6.1
Staff Development Curriculum

Staff Development Curriculum

School districts may select from the following workshops to customize a year-long staff development curriculum. These staff development offerings include the core curriculum—knowledge that every teacher and administrator should have to obtain a fundamental mastery of standards-based performance assessments. In addition, these offerings include an enrichment curriculum—workshops that are available on specific topics to assist teachers in the development and implementation of standards-based performance assessments for use in their classroom. Each workshop is scheduled for two hours. The workshops can also be extended and combined to allow additional hands-on participation. We can schedule workshops ranging in length from day long sessions to week long institutes. We can customize a Staff Development Plan to meet your needs. This is the kind of comprehensive staff development that the Center for Performance Assessment has implemented in school districts all across the country. More than just theory, our staff development focus provides practical, hands-on experience that moves the standards initiative in your district forward.

Core Curriculum

MSW 101

Why Standards?

Why Standards? Because they are fair and because they work! This course will present evidence in support of these ideas as well as introduce the legislative and educational rationale for standards. In addition, the fundamental differences between the standards-based approach to education and the traditional approaches as well as the differences between standards and norms will be discussed. The crucial issue of expectations—by teachers, by students, by parents and the community—is a vital component of standards-based education.

MSW 102

Goals for Classroom Assessment

This course identifies the criteria teachers will use to screen assignments and assessments used in their classrooms. It is designed to make the teacher a "critical consumer" of both outside materials and teacher created materials used for assignments and assessments. Practical suggestions will be presented to assist teachers in designing assignments and assessments that are challenging and engaging to students.

(continued)

figure 6.1

Staff Development Curriculum (continued)

MSW 103

Introduction to Performance Assessment

This course introduces the form and construction of performance assessments. Are all 'alternative assessments' performance assessments? This question as well as others will be answered. This course is designed to assist teachers with the integration of assessment and instructional practice in the classroom. The differences between traditional and performance assessment will be discussed. Practical applications for the classroom will be modeled including the identification of standards, activities and the evaluation criteria to be used to develop performance assessments.

MSW 104

Developing Scoring Guides

This course focuses on the development of meaningful, specific, and mutually exclusive scoring guides (rubrics) for performance assessment. The question, "Why use scoring guides?" will be answered. Sample scoring guides will be critiqued and suggestions will be offered to assist teachers in the creation of scoring guides. The extended version offers participants the opportunity to create a scoring guide to be used in their classroom.

MSW 105

Portfolio Assessment

This course focuses on the design, assembly, and scoring of portfolios. A distinction is made between a student's "working file" and a portfolio that is used to demonstrate proficiency in relation to standards. Practical ideas will be offered to increase the effectiveness of the portfolio as an assessment instrument.

MSW 106

Grading and Standards—Working Together

This course addresses the issues involved with incorporating standards-based performance and traditional grades. What kinds of changes need to be made in a traditional grading system to reflect a student's level of proficiency, not just their "letter" grade? A Standards Achievement Report will be discussed.

MSW 107

Equity Issues in Assessment

This course focuses on the imperative of equity in assessment design and the creation of "opportunities to learn" for all students. This course will include a discussion of principles of equity, as well as the importance of variable time and fixed learning for all students. Suggestions will be offered to assist teachers in maintaining equity in their classrooms and in their teaching practices. Examples of assessment strategies and accommodations in assessment will be discussed.

MSW 108

Designing Performance Assessments

This course considers the practical issues of the construction and evaluation of performance assessments. Ten steps to creating effective performance assessments will be presented and modeled. The participants will begin the construction of their own performance assessment.

(continued)

figure 6.1

Staff Development Curriculum (continued)

MSW 109

Technology, Assessment, and Standards

This course focuses on ways of using technology in the assessment process and for implementing standards. How can teachers use existing technology to help improve instruction, to make lessons more engaging for students, and to facilitate the integration of assessment into the instructional process? Specific ideas will be presented to help decrease the level of anxiety often associated with discussions of technology.

MSW 110

Designing a Standards–Based Classroom

This course will describe how a standards-based classroom differs from a traditional classroom. Specific strategies will be presented to help teachers make standards-based education a reality in their classroom. Suggestions for involving students in standards implementation will be discussed. The classroom becomes an environment in which learning is the focus for everyone, not simply the teacher teaching and the students learning.

MSW 111

Beyond Bloom—Learning Performance at High Levels of Application

This course will describe the importance of real world applications in teaching and learning. Students are more likely to stay engaged in the learning process when we increase the relevancy of instructional tasks. This becomes imperative if we are to raise expectations for our students and provide opportunities for success. Suggestions will be presented to help teachers expand current curriculum, rather effortlessly, to reflect real world applications.

MSW 112

Designing Standards–Based Performance Assessments

This course presents a specific plan for designing standards-based performance assessments. Each step is clearly explained and then modeled for the participants. Participants are then encouraged to design their own performance assessments within the supportive environment offered in the workshop setting.

MSW 113

Teaching Strategies for Implementing Standards

This workshop will present the idea that teachers will need to expand their repertoire of teaching strategies if the implementation of standards will become a reality. Practical ideas will assist teachers in designing lesson plans that focus on student achievement and real world applications. How can we redesign our current instructional ideas to raise expectations for our students and provide them with the tools they will need to meet those expectations?

MSW 114

Aligning Curriculum and Instruction to Standards

This workshop presents a model for aligning existing curriculum with standards. Hallmarks of effective standards-based instruction will be discussed as well as instructional planning that will provide students with the "Opportunity to Learn." Practical ideas that address the seamless integration between curriculum, instruction and assessment will be discussed. The next step is to design or to craft instruction that is aligned with both the curriculum and standards. The role of resources, both traditional and electronic, will be discussed.

figure 6.2
Staff Development Enrichment Curriculum

Enrichment Curriculum

Assignments and Assessments—These workshops focus on specific subject areas and specific grade levels to assist teachers in creating standards-based performance assessments and classroom assignments in specialized areas for immediate use by the participants.

MSW 201	Elementary Math
MSW 202	Elementary Language Arts
MSW 203	Elementary Science
MSW 204	Elementary Social Studies
MSW 205	Elementary Multi-Disciplinary
MSW 206	Middle School Math
MSW 207	Middle School Language Arts
MSW 208	Middle School Science
MSW 209	Middle School Social Studies
MSW 210	Middle School Multi-Disciplinary
MSW 211	High School Math
MSW 212	High School Language Arts
MSW 213	High School Science
MSW 214	High School Social Studies
MSW 215	High School Multi-Disciplinary

For additional information, please call:

Donna M. Davis, M.Ed.
Director, Professional Development
(800) THINK-99 ▪ (303) 504-9312

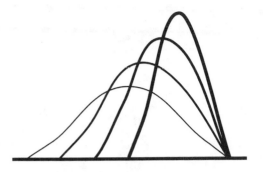

chapter seven

The Role of the Principal

Principals today are under siege. While teachers feel overwhelmed with the multiple demands of students, parents, and administrators, principals must respond to an even greater number of constituencies. When the suggestion is made that these men and women should be the educational leaders of their schools, some scoff and reply, "I spend from 7:00 a.m. until 7:00 p.m. on paperwork and discipline. If I'm not completely exhausted at that point, perhaps I'll devote an hour or two to educational leadership."

Despite their workload and the intense pressure of their jobs, principals have an enormous impact on the school environment. A number of studies, as well as careful observations by people who have spent much of their professional lives around schools, confirm this fundamental truth: even when the budgets, faculty, and students are the same, a change in a single person—the principal—can have a profound impact on the morale, enthusiasm, and educational environment of a school.

▓ Seven Steps for Principals

Principals who believe in the promise of standards can have a dynamic impact on making standards work. If the implementation of standards is regarded as "just one more initiative from the central office," it is unlikely to result in more than the most superficial response. The paperwork will be completed, but the classroom will be unaffected. This chapter suggests seven practical steps by which effective school leaders can jump-start the standards implementation process:

- Understand the standards

- Identify faculty leaders

- Create professional development opportunities

- Assess student progress

- Analyze classroom activity

- Recognize outstanding performance

- Reflect, revise, and improve

■ Understand the Standards

First, take time to become acquainted with your state and district standards, particularly those relating to the grade levels of your school. Perhaps your first reaction will be, "we're already doing this!" If so, great. Then you can use standards as a tool for communicating with parents and the public about what you are teaching. However, you may notice in some of your classrooms there are differences between what is actually happening and what the standards describe. Some teachers in your school may also note that textbooks do not include all the content described in the standards. Noticing these disparities is an essential step toward becoming a standards-based school. If you have not already provided every faculty member with a complete set of state and district standards, you should take immediate steps to do so. It is also up to the principal to carefully distinguish between claims to standards adoption and the real thing. Teachers who are simply tough and award high grades sparingly may or may not have "high standards"—it's at least possible that they simply have tests that effectively separate students from one another. A commitment to standards implies that the teacher is creating and using techniques to allow all students to meet standards—not maintaining the status quo in which only a few students are expected to do so.

Before plunging into professional development activities, the first step is to relax, sit down, and read the standards. Everyone in the building should have a working knowledge of the standards. Teachers need to know all the standards—not just those for their grade levels. It is very important for teachers to place their instruction into context. What will be expected at the next level of education? What should have been done before the student came to my class? Finally, it is imperative to share the standards with students and parents. It may be appropriate to transform the typically voluminous standards document into bite-sized pieces for distribution to the public. This may take place over the course of several weeks, during which you and the teachers in the school emphasize the standards for a particular area. By the end of the school year, however, a concerted effort should be made to communicate all of the standards to all parents and students.

◼ Identify Faculty Leaders

Experienced principals know that when implementing any change, the top-down method (changes mandated and enforced from the management) is rarely effective. Rather, systemic change occurs when faculty members emulate the success of their colleagues. It is, therefore, essential that the principal identify faculty leaders who have already accepted the principle that standards-based education is appropriate, important, and vital to the health of our schools. Take some time to nurture these leaders, and ensure that they share a common vision with you and the leadership of your district.

It is important to note that the faculty leaders in standards may not be the traditional faculty leaders who have been committee chairs and organizational leaders in the past. Rather, you want to identify innovative leaders. These are people who lead others not with the power of personality or organization alone, but with the power of ideas. Neither age nor experience is a criterion here. Teachers almost invariably know who the most effective educators are, and although they may not agree with everything these teachers do, effective educators are the ones who earn respect and, ultimately, emulation. If you are new to the building and want to find out who the most effective educators are, just ask—you are likely to find a strong consensus of opinion.

Once you have identified these faculty leaders, they must be nurtured and appreciated. Although extra money is seldom available to recognize exceptional performance and risk-taking leadership by faculty members, principals can find a number of other means to nurture and appreciate faculty leaders. Time for collaboration (perhaps facilitated by the principal taking the class for a couple of hours), extraordinary professional development opportunities, letters of recommendation for awards, public recognition of ideas and programs, and personal notes and letters are all ways in which effective principals show their appreciation for faculty leaders. Principals know better than many people how lonely leadership can be. When teachers are willing to accept the burden of leadership for the implementation of standards, the teachers deserve support, empathy, and every bit of assistance the principal can manage.

◼ Create Professional Development Opportunities

If we have learned anything in the past few decades of ill-fated educational reform efforts, it is that "professional development" in the traditional form has not worked. This used to mean hauling all faculty members into a meeting, entertaining them, pleading with them, finally ordering them to "reform" and, at last, sitting by helplessly while things continue to function just as they always have.

Standards-based professional development opportunities must be different. First, these opportunities do not occur in isolation, but must be part of a curriculum (see Chapter 6). Second, professional development is not uniformly provided to every teacher, but rather different levels of professional development are provided to different teachers depending on their background and familiarity with standards. The sample Staff Development Curriculum (pages 52-55) can be of great help with this. By the end of a two-year cycle, every teacher should have completed the learning objectives of such a curriculum, but not every teacher will have necessarily participated in every element of the curriculum. By taking the time to specifically allocate professional development resources based on the needs and backgrounds of teachers, you not only grant these people the professional respect they deserve, but you also conserve scarce staff development resources.

■ Assess Student Progress

The most certain way to kill a standards-based approach to education is to establish a wall between standards and assessments. Such a wall is erected when school leaders spend the months of September through March talking about standards. Then, in April, they make students and teachers endure the same tests which they have always taken—tests which may or may not be related in any form to the content standards you have been swearing will be the core of educational practice in your school.

To show that standards-based assessments are truly different, do not wait until April to start assessments. Ask every teacher in the building, over the course of the next month, to develop just one standards-based assignment (see Part Four for several models). Then allocate plenty of class time to complete these assignments. Identify how well your students are performing on just the standards associated with this assignment. If this is started early in the school year and continues throughout the year, a persuasive case can be made that the traditional "week of terror" associated with tests is irrelevant, inappropriate, and dispensable. You will also be able to make the persuasive case to parents and policy makers that by eliminating those tests, you are not reducing the amount of meaningful assessment in your school, but increasing it by a wide margin. Documents such as the Standards Achievement Report (see Chapter 9) can also help you make this case.

■ Analyze Classroom Activity

One of the best school superintendents I know, Dr. Stan Scheer, astounded his colleagues (and, he might admit, himself) when he put himself on the substitute teacher list for his district. In this way, he learned more about what was happening in his district's classrooms than he would have learned in a thousand committee meetings and formal presentations. He learned how hard teachers work, how profound the social and family problems are, and how primary grade teachers simply never have a break during the morning hours—not even to use the restroom! During the too typically brief observations, which administrators usually make of classrooms, there is always some activity going on. But during the sort of extended observations made by Dr. Scheer, it was also obvious that a lot of time is wasted by the interference of outside forces, and even some of the planned activities did not really relate to the educational objectives of his district.

But don't administrators need time to plan and think? In fact, it was only by spending extended time in the classroom that Dr. Scheer was able to systematically think about what was really happening in the classroom. These hours allowed him to encourage teachers to challenge themselves to pull the weeds before planting the flowers—that is, to identify classroom activities that can be eliminated in order to make room for substantive standards-based activities. Teachers tend to listen to a leader who has walked in their shoes not years ago, but days ago.

It is fair to note that some leadership professors object to the idea of a school leader getting so involved with individual classrooms. They believe that there is a "role" assigned to the principal and superintendent, and that a violation of that role intrudes on the teachers' areas of responsibilities. It might even indicate that the teachers are not trusted by administrators who choose to make such extended observations. Such a view, in my judgment, does not conform to today's classroom reality. My conversations with thousands of teachers and hundreds of administrators indicate that the traditional assumptions about the role of school leaders must be challenged. Effective decisions require accurate information, and the statistics delivered to principals and superintendents are not sufficient. There is no substitute for personal observations of hours, not minutes.

You will not analyze classroom activities with a questionnaire or a faculty meeting. You need to be there—without beeper or cellular phone—completely present in the classroom, down on the floor if necessary, interacting with students and teachers, and perhaps even reminding yourself why you entered this profession in the first place.

■ Recognize Outstanding Performance

In the course of analyzing classroom activities, many wonderful things will happen, but perhaps the best is that you will have the opportunity to immediately recognize and appreciate outstanding performance. You probably already have some teachers who have created their own standards-based assignments, who regularly fill in the gaps left by textbooks, and who have developed multi-disciplinary assignments that are engaging, interesting, and absorbing for the students. You will see creative ways of dealing with incessant interruptions and disturbances, and you will see an intense focus on academic achievement. Because these images are so contrary to the public image of the classroom, it is imperative that you recognize and publicize these educational heroes. If your work rules and resources permit it, monetary rewards are nice. But never underestimate the power of the personal note, the public recognition, the picture sent to the newspaper, or the commendation placed in a personnel file. Administrators are required to find the time to fill a book with paper when it comes time to reprimand or fire a teacher; a commendation takes only a single page.

■ Reflect, Revise, and Improve

Principals must walk the talk of standards. One way of doing this is to systematically reflect on how far your school has come, and how far it has yet to travel down the road toward standards implementation. A public display of your "standards implementation report" and a visual indicator of the progress since your last report a few months ago will send an important message. This message says very clearly, "I am expecting students and teachers to be accountable for the implementation of standards only after I have become accountable for their implementation." The seven steps in this chapter are just the start—but they are the first steps on a very rewarding journey.

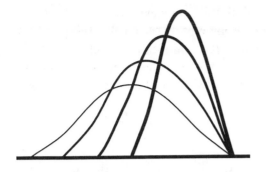

chapter eight

The Role of the District

Superintendents and board of education members have some of the most difficult jobs in the country. Their tenures are notoriously brief and their public esteem is frequently low. Their critics include people who are quite convinced they could do the job better themselves, but who typically have not spent a millisecond in the shoes of those they so vehemently criticize. When board members and superintendents accept the challenge of implementing standards, they have done far more than simply given their approval to the latest educational reform initiative. They have, instead, committed themselves and their districts to comprehensive and rigorous courses of action which will influence teaching and learning for decades to come. This chapter outlines six key responsibilities of superintendents and board members as they seek to make standards work.

■ Ownership

Standards cannot be the product of the "educational experts." Instead, standards must have broad ownership from every major constituency within the community. Even if your state has already adopted standards, each local district typically has the responsibility to also develop its own standards that are at least as challenging as the state standards.

The constituencies that should be represented in the standards development process include, at the very least, the following: teachers, parents, community members, business owners and managers, colleges and universities, groups representing significant minority populations in the community, unions, and school administrators. The local history of your district may dictate the inclusion of other key interest groups. In many communities, for example, the American Association of Retired Persons (AARP) is a key voting group for school bond issues, and it would ill-behoove any school district to exclude this group from any major policy initiative. Indeed, research on school bond elections indicates that support from the population frequently hinges on a clear understanding that voting "yes" will result in clearly understood educational results. Community ownership of standards is an excellent means to achieve this broadly based understanding.

■ Congruence

The superintendent and board of education must ensure that the policies they implement involving standards are congruent with other policy initiatives undertaken by the school system. In fact, the litmus test for every other educational initiative in the district should be, "Does this conform with our commitment to standards?" This means that in the selection of textbooks and assessment instruments, conformity to district standards is essential. I know of one district in which a national assessment instrument vendor reviewed every single item in the assessment to determine the correspondence of those elements to the district's standards. This is in marked contrast to the bland assertions of textbook and assessment vendors that their products are, "of course, standards-based."

Congruence must also be assured in personnel decisions. As superintendents and other senior administrators contemplate the hiring, promotion, and tenure of teachers, administrators, and other key decision-makers, the issue of standards must be part of these conversations. There are a number of fine teachers and administrators who do not believe in standards or who believe that they are a passing fad of minor significance. There are many places in the country for these people to work—but your district is not one of them. Because this statement can be regarded by many as inflammatory, let me elaborate.

Standards are not just a good idea—they are essential. They are essential not only for educational effectiveness; they are required for educational equity. If a school had a math teacher who was completely competent, but who sincerely believed that Hispanic children couldn't do algebra, few superintendents or school boards would hesitate to terminate the teacher. (Few people would argue, "Every teacher has the right to his opinion, and all opinions on the mushy field of education are equally valid.") In this hypothetical case, we would conclude that competence in math isn't enough—the teacher must also be able to teach all students without prejudice.

What about a teacher who refuses to take a standards-based approach to education? Is this just a matter of personal opinion and professional independence? If we accept these tired claims based on a twisted notion of professionalism, then any teacher can say, "I can teach the math, and it's the students' responsibility to learn the way that I teach." If such a statement is equated with professional independence, then there is little recourse against the teacher who explicitly confesses a prejudice based on ethnicity or gender. In sum, teachers have a responsibility to teach and leaders have a responsibility to make decisions based on the best interests of students. If we fail to lead decisively, then teachers who took the risks and endured the work of implementing standards will soon get the message that the words of their leaders are not congruent with their actions.

Congruence is also essential in the use of external evaluations. The discipline of educational evaluation has too frequently depended on the notion of expertise—that is, the designated "expert" evaluates a program based on her individual understanding of what is good and proper rather than the criteria of the district. In a standards-based district, however, the standards have already set the criteria for evaluation, and hence every external evaluator should be expected to develop familiarity with district standards. More importantly, it should be clear in every Request For Proposal (RFP) for external evaluations that the standards of the district—not the prejudices of the consultant—will be the definitive guide for the evaluation.

▦ Experimentation

One of the most frustrating things for superintendents and board members is the feeling of utter impotence as they implement a policy initiative and then watch as nothing happens. Harry Truman remarked that when General Dwight Eisenhower assumed the Presidency, Ike would be immensely frustrated by the contrast to his military days in which every order was followed by a salute and an action. As President, Truman observed, the most powerful man on earth is frequently powerless in the face of the immovable federal bureaucracy.

Systemic change rarely occurs as the result of an order, a resolution, or a policy. Rather, changes in complex systems occur when the multiple key decision-makers (in this case, teachers, principals, students, and parents) decide that the new initiative is in their best interest. This conclusion will be reached most frequently by these many decision-makers, not on the basis of a persuasive speech by the superintendent, but rather by their direct observations of the use of standards in classrooms and schools they know to be effective. As a result, the use of a pilot program is essential to standards implementation at the district level.

Superintendents are typically action-oriented leaders—that is how they became superintendents. Some of them, along with many board members who must stand for reelection in a short period of time, might ask, "If standards are so great, why not simply implement them throughout the district immediately? A pilot project just seems like a waste of time!" This question deserves a serious response.

1. **Pilot projects create enthusiasm among the key faculty leaders and principals.**

   The best educational innovators in your district have probably already been implementing some version of standards already, and it is essential that they be on your team.

2. **Pilot projects allow the initial bugs to be worked out of a system which lowers the costs due to errors.**

   Many initial drafts of standards, including those approved at the state level, contain important omissions. Other drafts are not as clear as they should be. The pilot project allows a district to have the second draft of standards implemented on a district-wide level, with the omissions and ambiguities corrected prior to large-scale implementation. Experienced computer users know that you "never buy version 1.0 of anything." The same applies to district-wide implementation of standards—first work out the bugs with a pilot project.

3. **The justification for pilot projects is leverage.**

   There is an enormous professional development process involved in standards imple-mentation (see Chapter 6). This challenge can best be achieved through the use of teachers teaching teachers. The participants in your pilot project will have local credibility and direct experience in making standards work in your district. In addition, the use of outside consultants can be focused on a fewer number of schools in workshops of a manageable size.

4. **Pilot schools provide an ideal long-term source of mentors for student teachers.**

   Few teacher training institutions are providing any in-depth preparation for standards-based performance assessments. If this is a skill you expect teachers in your district to have, then it is essential that you build that expectation into the student teacher training program, and that student teachers are not assigned to mentor teachers who are not actively conducting their classes in accordance with the district's academic content standards.

5. **The use of pilot programs gives the district leadership the opportunity to provide public recognition and rewards for those who are leaders in the standards movement.**

   To create systemic change, you must change the system of rewards. This includes not only appropriate remuneration for the extra meetings and time a pilot project entails, but also includes public recognition, professional development resources, and special consideration for promotion and advancement. One of the most certain ways to effectively kill standards implementation in your district is for the leadership to talk about the wonders of innovation and academic standards, and then give the Teacher of the Year award to the person whose class had the best test scores on an assessment not related to your district standards.

■ Support—Time, Money, and Protection

Time

Requests for support probably constitute 90 percent of a superintendent's in-box. Standards implementation requires support in three specific ways—time, money, and protection. Management theorist Tom Peters has remarked that if he wanted to see what a leader's priorities were, he would look no farther than the leader's calendar. If the days were consumed with meetings and presentations, then the headquarters staff (invariably large) would be devoting its time and resources to preparation and elaborate presentation for those meetings. If, by contrast, the days were largely consumed with community associations, boards, and public posturing, then the leader was probably using the organization to promote his own image rather than using his leadership skills to promote the organization. Finally, if the leader was spending time doing what the organization actually did (make cars, sell toys, teach students) then, (and only then) was the leader devoting the precious resource of time where it belonged.

Surely no superintendent can get through many days without meetings of some kind. But my observation is that too many school leaders are captives, rather than controllers, of their calendars. If school leaders are to provide the time essential for standards implementation, they must devote significant amounts of time for teacher collaboration. This is not simply a longer "planning period" but rather a specifically structured time in which the specific elements of student performance standards are reviewed. Some school districts that are successfully implementing standards devote two to four hours every week to this effort. Just as Peters advocates a minimum of four hours each week of "management by wandering around," the superintendent focused on standards should similarly allocate a minimum of four hours each week to the subject of standards. Some of this time could be spent watching teachers in a pilot project struggle with their evaluation of student work. Other hours could be spent with members of the business community improving their understanding and support for the standards movement in the district. Still other hours could be spent in extended classroom observation, sitting on the floor for at least a couple of hours, with some second graders.

The superintendent must be able to articulate what makes a standards-based classroom different. In one standards-focused district, the superintendent required every senior district-level administrator, including the superintendent, to create and teach a block of standards-based instruction. This leader is putting his time where his rhetoric is.

Money

Support for standards by the district also means money. Specifically, standards implementation requires blocks of time (typically half a day per week) for teachers to review student work, create scoring guides,[6] and create new standards-based assignments. Allocating this time will cost money. Given the workload of most teachers, their pursuit of graduate degrees in their non-working hours, their family responsibilities, and the stress associated with a normal school day, it is unreasonable to expect that this half-day block should occur after the school day or on weekends. (I have, however, seen some effective standards implementation teams do this, but the participants ended the school year physically and mentally exhausted.) The best course of action is for the district to provide either long-term substitutes or other organized activities for the classrooms of these teachers so that the teachers can

---

6. Scoring Guide describes the document used to determine whether the work is exemplary, proficient, progressing toward the standard, or not yet meeting the standard. A Standards Achievement Report (SAR) is an example of one such guide. These topics are covered in more detail in Chapters 9 and 17.

spend these half-day blocks at a consistent time and day, and they can devote their full intellectual energy to the hard work of standards implementation.

Protection

Finally, the support required of the superintendent and board is that of protection of the champions of standards. The resistance to standards implementation can be formidable and emotionally draining. This is particularly true at the secondary school level, where some students will spend more hours and take more classes, than has traditionally been the case in order to meet their requirement to demonstrate proficiency in all of the district standards. With more hours devoted to academic content standards, there will be fewer hours devoted to non-academic pursuits. Inevitably, some non-academic classes and popular extra-curricular activities will suffer.

■ Leading Reluctant Followers

When a district changes its orientation from seat time to the achievement of standards, it often takes more time for many students to achieve these standards. This leaves some teachers, parents, and students asking, with quavering voices, "Do you mean to tell me what I've been doing all these years isn't valuable because it doesn't meet the district's new standards?" The only response to this query is, "Your work is indeed valuable, because every class and activity including yours (for example, drama, music, art, woodworking, etc.), will now be linked to an academic standard. How can you enrich this class so that it will help our students achieve standards?" Some teachers and parents will respond, "But this just isn't an academic class, and never has been!"

Faced with absolute intransigence, the superintendent and board must unhesitatingly make the decision to eliminate those activities or to do them in a strikingly different way. While such a position makes some vocational educators very apprehensive, others are delighted that their classes will at last be recognized as academic. They know from experience that many students (particularly those who are kinesthetic learners) can learn fractions, decimals, ratios, and many mathematical standards in home economics, industrial arts, and music classes. There are many students who will learn these standards far better in such a "hands-on" class than they will in a traditional abstract math class. But some programs supported only by tradition and popularity will have constituencies ready to conduct a wholesale attack on the standards movement.

The effective superintendent and board will have no choice but to take swift and sure action to protect the champions of standards from these attacks and, ultimately, to eliminate inappropriate, unproductive, and wasteful activities from the district.

■ Focus

The final obligation of district leadership is focus. Initially, the school board should seriously consider a one-year moratorium on any new initiatives in the twelve months following the implementation of standards. Implementation of standards is a mammoth project and no complex system should attempt to undertake multiple major changes, particularly if there is a risk that some of the changes are contradictory. In addition, the board and superintendent should build into every agenda a progress report on standards implementation. This should specifically include an action report at the building and classroom level, where particularly effective examples of standards implementation can receive a high level of recognition and appreciation. Just as many board agendas begin with the Pledge of Allegiance and public recognition, so the standards-driven district will give consistent attention and priority to reports of successful standards implementation.

The leadership must ensure broad community ownership of standards. The content of meetings includes more than the words of the participants. Public wall charts in the board and superintendent meeting rooms, containing standards achievement reports for the district and individual schools, will also send a powerful message as these documents receive wide public attention. To implement standards effectively, educational leaders must do more than pass resolutions and articulate policies. They must insist that all policies of the district are congruent, and that the district standards are the filter through which all other policies must pass to ensure a high level of consistency. Leaders must experiment with the early phases of standards implementation and use pilot programs to demonstrate the effectiveness of standards in their district. Support by leaders, including time, money, and protection, is essential in the standards-driven district. Finally, leaders must focus on standards, not only by eliminating distractions, but by providing consistent attention, in meeting agendas and environments, to the district's focus on standards.

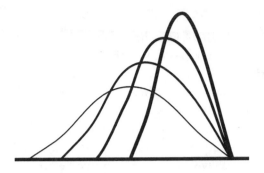

chapter nine

Measuring Standards Achievement

In a standards based system the Standards Achievement Report (SAR) becomes the alternative to the traditional report card (or at the very least, a supplement to the traditional report card). The traditional methods of measuring student achievement have included standardized tests and report cards. In Chapter 3, the shortcomings of norm-referenced standardized tests were compared to the advantages offered by the standards-based approach to educational assessment. These comparisons are summarized in Figure 9.1.

figure 9.1

Standards-Based Assessments vs. Norms-Based Assessments

Comparison of Assessment Methods

Standards

1. Standards are fixed.
2. Standards are cooperative.
3. Standards measure proficiency.
4. Standards promote mixed ability grouping.
5. Standards are challenging.
6. Standards are complicated.
7. Standards address causes, intermediate effects, and achievement.

Norms

1. Norms move.
2. Norms are competitive.
3. Norms (and their counterparts, grades) measure behavior.
4. Norms promote segregation of students by ability.
5. Norms provide excuses for a "dumbed down" curriculum.
6. Norms are simple.
7. Norms reflect only test scores.

The traditional report card suffers many of the same deficiencies as norm-based assessments. These deficiencies are particularly pronounced for teachers who have been trained (or perhaps required) to grade on the curve—that is, assigning grades not on the basis of student performance alone, but on the basis of student performance compared to other students. The traditional report card does not rely on norms, but simply upon the teacher's judgments regarding the student's ability, along with test results, homework assignments, classroom behavior, timeliness of assignments, neatness, and other matters that inevitably enter into the recipe for determining grades. Can the implementation of standards help make this document more meaningful and less terrorizing? I believe so. As an alternative to the traditional report card, consider the use of the Standards Achievement Report (SAR), Figure 9.2, page 79. (The Standards Achievement Report [SAR] will be explained in more detail later in this chapter.)

■ The Accountability Imperative

Parents demand many things from the public schools, some are reasonable and some are not. It is reasonable, for example, for parents to demand that schools provide their children with challenging and decent educational opportunities. It is manifestly unreasonable, by contrast, for parents to demand (as an astonishing number do) that schools provide their children with values and morals, but, they quickly add, "make sure you don't talk about any political, religious, ethical, moral, or value issues with which I disagree. And while you're at it, make up for the neglect the child suffered during the first five years of life, straighten out his behavioral problems, and for goodness sake do something about his terrible table manners."

■ A Fair Question: "How's My Kid Doing In School?"

This caricature only slightly exaggerates the frustrations felt by many teachers and educational leaders when dealing with public sentiment, which often borders on contempt, toward education. Perhaps the most reasonable demand of parents, however, is that schools provide a coherent response to the question, "How is my child doing in school?" I submit that sending home the mysterious results of a norm-referenced test on the last day of school is close to educational malpractice. This leads to meaningless exchanges such as "I got a 136—what did you get?" and damaging conclusions such as "You missed the program (perhaps gifted and talented, resource room, learning disabled, and so on) by only one point—we are so sorry." As reprehensible as is the technique of summing up a child's educational attainment with a single number on a test, the use of the traditional report card is not much better. Saying that Matilda's math performance is a "D+" suggests that she has some work to do this summer, but also suggests that she passed and is ready for the next grade. In fact, the "D+" could mean one of several things. Our conversations with teachers reveal that a final grade of "D+" could mean, among many other things:

- Matilda received average grades of 76 on all of her homework assignments and tests.

- Matilda does not understand the material at all, but she tries very hard, behaves well in class, and her earnestness has impressed the teacher so that a passing grade is appropriate. The "D+" is the teacher's attempt to provide Matilda with some self-esteem, which the teacher understands is important for "slow" children like Matilda.

- Matilda excels at math and is perhaps the brightest student in class. But she repeatedly turns in her homework assignments late and is missing some assignments entirely. The "point system" used by the teacher, which was announced at the beginning of the school year, penalizes students for missing assignments.

- "Matilda is just not responsible," the teacher concludes, "Perhaps getting a 'D+' will teach her a lesson."

- Be honest, the teacher simply does not like Matilda, and Matilda makes it quite clear that the feeling is mutual.

The list could go on and on. The point is parents frequently do not know what a "D+," or any other grade, really means. The conventional letter grade system certainly does not answer the question "How is my child doing?" Moreover, the system for awarding grades might include student behavior, timeliness, neatness, and many other considerations. The grading system may change drastically from one class to another. Thus the notion of adding grades together to arrive at the much-vaunted GPA (Grade Point Average) makes as much sense as averaging the number of pounds of weight, inches of height, and points of IQ to come up with an HCA (Human Characteristic Average).[7] Such a computation would be meaningless and silly and would never be taken seriously. Yet we compare the incomparable—grades from different classes—without substantial questioning about their intended meaning.

■ The Alternative—The Standards Achievement Report (SAR)

If report cards and grades fail to respond to the reasonable demand of parents for accountability, then what is the answer? Several schools across the country are using the Standards Achievement Report (SAR) as a supplement to, or replacement for, the traditional report card, and initially it should always be used just as a supplement, not a replacement. An example of the Standards Achievement Report is provided in Figure 9.2.

Ideally, the Standards Achievement Report (SAR) should be printed on a file folder, with the four surfaces of the folder allocated to the four core academic areas of language, math,

---

7. Howard Gardner has articulated the theory of multiple intelligences. His research indicates that there are a multiplicity of intelligences, including spatial, musical, and interpersonal intelligence, to name a few. His research also indicates that there is no relationship between the IQ as measured by traditional intelligence tests and the existence of other types of intelligence. Daniel Goleman has more recently articulated the idea of emotional intelligence and offers persuasive evidence that this is more important for future success than traditional test scores.

science, and social studies. Inside the file are documents—assignments, assessments, teacher observations, student reflections—that support the conclusions in the SAR on the front of the folder.

Figure 9.2 (page 79) provides an example of what one page of the SAR might look like. In the left-hand column are abbreviated performance standards for that academic content area. Please note that these are abbreviated; the full standards should be given to each student and parent at the beginning of the school year. In the next column is an indication of the student's performance on that standard. The same numbering system—4, exceeds the standard (exemplary); 3, meets the standard (proficient); 2, progressing toward the standard; and 1, not meeting the standard—should be used on all papers and reports. At the bottom there is plenty of space for remarks by the teacher.

In a realistic SAR, several rows will be blank, indicating that the student has not yet attempted this standard. But, by the end of a designated point in schooling (typically fourth, eighth, and twelfth grades), each student should have completed every one of the standards with a rating of proficient or higher. Using the same SAR through each continuum of grades (K–4, 5–8, and 9–12), both students and parents have a clear idea of the student's strengths and weaknesses, months and even years before the threshold years of fourth, eighth, and twelfth grades.

The use of the SAR clearly requires more effort by both the teacher and the parents. The payoff, however, is a quantum improvement in the level of clarity with which parents understand the educational progress of their children. This will not work if it is merely sent home in a child's back pack—the nearest thing in this solar system to a black hole. Teachers, students, and parents must discuss the SAR together and interpret its meaning. Together, the teacher-student-parent team can develop appropriate strategies, including the role of consistent and supportive encouragement and help from home.

From a building and district point of view, the aggregate of Standards Achievement Report data will allow administrators to identify with far greater precision the strengths and weaknesses of their curriculum and instruction programs. For example, rather than simply having a grade point average for middle school math students, administrators will know that there is a particular problem in the study of ratios and decimals in fourth and fifth grade classes. Instead of hearing reports of failures by ninth grade English students, curriculum strategists can identify issues in vocabulary and written expression in sixth and seventh graders. This makes the SAR a most effective communication tool (see Chapter 25 for more information about communicating with parents).

■ An Additional Alternative—The Computerized SAR

The Computerized Standards Achievement Report (CSAR), helps parents, teachers, principals, and school leaders answer the critical question, "How are we doing with respect to meeting our standards?" Only comprehensive and continuous standards-based performance assessments can answer that question. The Computerized Standards Achievement Report can quickly and efficiently analyze and report this information. The CSAR is available for either PC or Macintosh computer systems and uses either Microsoft Access or Apple ClarisWorks database software. Because the CSAR uses database software that many schools already have, the CSAR provides a cost-effective way for school systems to monitor the implementation of standards. Sample printouts are illustrated in Figures 9.4 and 9.5, pages 81-82.

■ What About Behavior?

One of the most frequent criticisms of the standards-based approach to education is that it emphasizes the achievement of standards without appropriate emphasis on the behavior of students. If a student is proficient in quadratic equations but never turns in assignments on time and is uncooperative in class, should the teacher be allowed to reflect dissatisfaction with such a student? Of course—parents should certainly know if their child is disorganized, late, uncooperative, or unpleasant. But they will rarely gather such information by intuition. Behavioral standards can be made explicit in a Standards Achievement Report just as academic standards can be explicit. If, in our earlier example, Matilda excels at math but not in the category so rarely observed in today's report cards, deportment, then the Standards Achievement Report allows the teacher to be explicit about Matilda's strengths and weaknesses. Moreover, such specificity helps avoid the tragedy of placing very bright students in remedial classrooms because their grades are low, only to discover (typically much later) that low grades reflected boredom, distraction, or breaches of decorum, rather than intellectual deficiencies.

■ This is Too Hard!

Another frequent criticism of the use of the Standards Achievement Report is that it is too detailed, time-consuming, and difficult. Precisely! Assessing the educational achievement of a child is detailed, time-consuming, and difficult. Two observations might help overcome this objection. First, teachers frequently have the documentation to justify the grades they assign. The vast majority of teachers are not arbitrary and capricious in their grading policies, but the documentation of precisely what lies behind the "B–" or "D+" is frequently known only to the teacher. Thus no matter how rational the grading policy might be, if it is shrouded in mystery, it appears irrational to parents, students, and the public. I would argue that if the documentation is readily available (and it usually is whenever a grade is challenged), then it makes much more sense to provide it in a format that makes clear how the student was evaluated.

Second, it is disgraceful that emotional and professional energy, as well as extraordinary financial resources, are inappropriately allocated to programs for children whose educational achievement has been "diagnosed" through poor grades. Thus we have the spectacle of school districts in which more than 50 percent of ninth grade students take an introductory math course more than once because a student who receives a "failing grade" must take it again to meet grade-based graduation requirements. Anecdotal evidence suggests that the vast majority of students (teachers estimate more than 70 percent) who repeat introductory high school math classes fall into one of two categories: (1) those who were never prepared in the first place for the class, or (2) those who failed because of attitudinal and behavioral reasons. In the case of the first group of students (those not prepared), a Standards Achievement Report from the previous year would have made it clear why the student required more preparation. Even if the student had a "passing grade of D+," the Standards Achievement Report would make clear why the student needed more preparation. It was not necessary to waste a year of time and resources forcing the student to receive a failing grade in order for him to finally get help.

What about the students with attitudinal and behavior problems? A Standards Achievement Report would document that their math proficiency was acceptable, but their conduct was not. Therefore, the appropriate strategy for these students is not to reinforce their bad behavior by allowing them to repeat the process of rebellion, but rather to place them in a class with a math content that is more challenging, using instructional strategies designed for disruptive students.

■ What About Parents?

Perhaps the greatest advantage of a Standards Achievement Report is the opportunity for parents to participate in the educational process of the child in an explicit and tangible way. Report cards typically provide a small space for the parent to sign the document and, occasionally, to provide one or two sentences of comments. Such opportunities for parental feedback usually expire in the late elementary grades. An effective Standards Achievement Report, by contrast, will include two critical pieces of information for parents. First, the report makes clear what standards the student has yet to achieve. Parents thus have the opportunity to do much more than say "do more math homework" but can work with their children on specific content areas. Second, the parents have the opportunity not only to sign the document, but to apply some standards to themselves.

Another page of the Standards Achievement Report folder might look something like Figure 9.3, page 80. The Standards Achievement Report folder sends the clear message that parents are critically important members of the educational team, and they should be as reflective about their own contribution to this team as are students and teachers. In this part of the report, parents respond to such standard questions as, "I review homework with my child every day," or "I limit the amount of television my child watches on school nights," or "I do not permit my child to have access to tobacco, drugs, or alcohol."

While parental responses are not a component of student evaluation and are not intended to be intrusive, they can help a teacher understand whether or not there is at least minimal engagement by parents in the educational performance of the child. Such a list also allows the parents to model for their children the importance of accountability and goal setting. The Standards Achievement Report reinforces the instrumental role of the parent in the educational success of the child.

Obviously, the content will vary with the age of the child, but it is my contention that if schools expect more parental involvement in the education of students, they must do more than ask parents to attend meetings, sell candy bars, and support the athletic teams. Rather, they must seek the direct involvement of parents in the daily educational activities of children.

Too frequently, the standards movement has been discussed only among administrators and teachers. The use of the Standards Achievement Report transforms the movement to one involving parents and students in a meaningful and tangible way. It makes standards a part of daily classroom practice as well as a part of the conversation between students and their parents. And perhaps most important of all, it makes the parental contribution to education explicit and accountable.

■ The Most Important Rule: Tell the Truth

In the course of my many opportunities to speak with groups of teachers, administrators, and parents, I am often asked to sum up the most important element of my standards and assessment philosophy. This book has 26 chapters, reproducible handouts, and sample performance assignments, and much remains unsaid. Nevertheless, when challenged to be concise about what effective standards and assessment are all about, I respond with three words: "Tell the truth." That is, indeed, the essence of effective standards and assessment. We tell the truth about what we expect of students. We tell the truth about the differences between their present performance and those standards. We tell the truth about the time and effort it will take to close that gap. And we tell the truth about the progress that students make toward the goals the community has established. Neither cryptic statistics nor percentiles nor evasive platitudes nor bromides about student self-esteem can meet this simple test of truth. Only a clear and direct statement about expectations and performance can meet such a test.

Unfortunately, the truth hurts. Many states are half-way through the standards movement—they have established their expectations of student performance, but tremble at the thought of telling the public about the difference between those expectations and the reality of student performance. They say that they want accountability, but what they report is a hodge-podge of test scores only distantly related to the standards that the community has adopted. Standards and assessment are inextricably linked. Standards without new assessments, new report cards, and new accountability systems are little more than castles in the air—lovely to contemplate but utterly without a foundation.

For school leaders and policy makers, telling the truth about standards, expectations, and performance will be difficult, but it might sound something like this:

> "We expect every student to read complex directions, write persuasively, and calculate competently. We expect every teacher to apply consistent standards, evaluate student performance accurately, and coach students with diligence and compassion. We expect every parent to support teachers

and students in their mutual quest for excellence. And we cannot afford, nor will we tolerate, practitioners or leaders who believe that failure is inevitable. We know that if a choice must be made between essential truth about student performance and the subordination of our standards to convenience, we will choose truth, however inconvenient, unpopular, or challenging it may be. We didn't engage in a rigorous program of academic standards because it was popular or because it was a fad. We took this course because it was the right thing to do. Educational progress can never happen without truth as its foundation, and it is to the wonderful truth of student potential and the challenging truth of student performance that we are unalterably committed."

figure 9.2
Standards Achievement Report

Standards

Language Arts	**4** Exemplary (Date)	**3** Proficient (Date)	**2** Progressing* (Date)	**1** Does Not Meet* (Date)
1. Write and speak for a variety of purposes and for diverse audiences.				
2. Write and speak using conventional grammar, usage, sentence structure, punctuation, capitalization, and spelling.				
3. Read and understand a variety of materials.				
4. Apply thinking skills to reading, writing, speaking, listening, and viewing.				
5. Read to locate, select, and make use of relevant information from a variety of media, reference, and technological sources.				
6. Read and recognize literature as an expression of human experience.				

Teacher Comments:

*Plan for Meeting Standards:

Parent Comments:

figure 9.3

Standards Achievement Report, Parent Contribution

Parent Contribution

		Never	Sometimes	Always
1.	We/I review homework every day.			
2.	We/I do not allow our child to have access to alcohol, tobacco, or drugs.			
3.	We/I restrict television viewing on school nights.			
4.	We/I enforce a bed time on school nights.			
5.	We/I read with our child at least three times a week.			
6.	We/I encourage our child to write letters.			
7.	We/I discuss current events with our child at least once each week.			

Comments:

figure 9.4

Computerized SAR (CSAR) #1

D. Bruce Thomas Elementary School
Quarterly Standards Proficiency Report

Standard 2: Communicate effectively, using written, verbal, and artistic forms, and appreciate the creative expression of others.

Classroom		Percent of Students				
Grade	Teacher	Exemplary	Proficient	Progressing	Not Meeting Standard	Not Attempted
1	Mrs. Jones	10	85	5		
	Miss Williams		70	15	15	
2	Mr. Baker	5	88	2	5	
	Mrs. Mbise		92	3	5	
3	Mrs. Davis		90	10		
	Dr. Bruce	15	75	5	5	
4	Mrs. Alexander		65	10	25	
	Ms. Lawrence	3	92	5		
	Ms. Doe	5	90	5		
5	Mr. Reeves	8	74	8	5	5
	Mrs. Ellis		68	20	12	
6	Mrs. Parker	5	85	10		
	Mr. Young	5	79	16		

Percentage of Students Meeting Standards

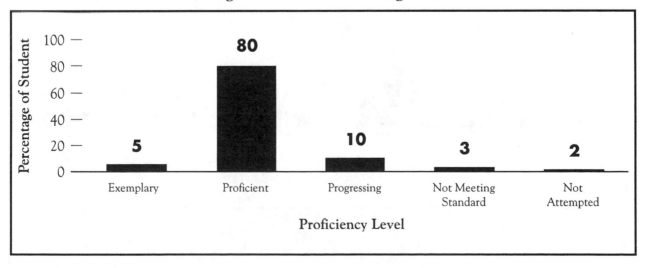

figure 9.5

Computerized SAR (CSAR) #2

District Summary
Quarterly Standards Proficiency Report

Standard 2: Communicate effectively, using written, verbal, and artistic forms, and appreciate the creative expression of others.

School		Percent of Students				
Building	Teacher	Exemplary	Proficient	Progressing	Not Meeting Standard	Not Attempted
Alice Bay	Mrs. Jones	10	85	5		
D. Bruce Thomas	Miss Williams		70	15	15	
Green Valley	Mr. Baker	5	88	2	5	
Hawkins	Mrs. Mbise		92	3	5	
Lehigh Estates	Mrs. Davis		90	10		
Donna Miller	Dr. Bruce	15	75	5	5	
Perkins Valley	Mrs. Alexander		65	10	25	
Justice Douglas	Ms. Lawrence	3	92	5		

Percentage of Students Meeting Standards

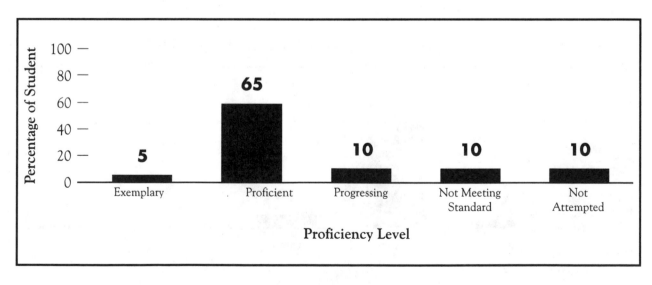

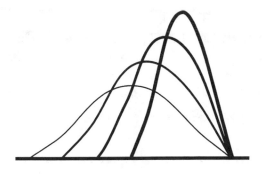

chapter ten

Validity and Reliability

The fundamental requirements of any assessment in any form include validity and reliability. Although these terms are used quite commonly, they are frequently misunderstood. The purpose of this chapter is to identify what validity and reliability mean in the context of standards-based performance assessments.

■ Validity and Reliability—What Is the Difference?

In order for a measure to be reliable, it must be consistent. For example, imagine that I am stepping on a scale at the doctor's office. The first time I step on the scale, it shows that I weigh 250 pounds. The second time I step on the scale, just a moment later, it shows 200 pounds, and the third time I step on the scale, it reads 150 pounds. This lack of consistency—or lack of reliability—means that although the physician may have had good medical reasons for wanting to know my weight, she was using an unreliable instrument—in this case a faulty scale. Her diagnosis might have ranged from obesity to anorexia, depending on which reading of the scale the physician decided to use. Therefore reliability is the first issue when considering any measurement. The physician clearly had a sound reason to know my weight, but she was using the wrong instrument to measure it.

Too frequently, in the context of education, we let our desire for information overwhelm our inhibitions against using faulty and unreliable instruments. Because we earnestly want to know how a student performs in mathematics, we administer tests; however, those tests are often inconsistent and unreliable. We justify the use of terrible tests because we want to know the information and we have been directed by the political powers to determine how students are performing in mathematics. After all, the label on the booklet said "math test" just as the label on the instrument in the doctor's office said "scale." But we cannot evaluate the reliability of the instrument based on its label or our need for information. Rather, we must evaluate the reliability of the instrument based on its demonstrated consistency in providing information to us. With no changes in my food consumption, I should be able to mount the scale three times within a few minutes of each other and get very similar results. Likewise, I should be able to administer the math test to the same individual and, regardless of other influences on that person, get similar results. If I do not, then I do not have a reliable instrument.

■ Reliability Is Not Enough

Unfortunately, even the most precise scale is not enough if what I really want to measure is my blood sugar. If I had a scale that scientists assured me was "reliable" to within one millionth of a pound, it would not do my doctor much good if she was attempting to identify problems with my eyesight, my blood sugar, malignant tumors, or any number of other ailments which were not related to my weight.

Our use of reliable (that is consistent) tests in education is similar to a student getting on a very accurate scale and the teacher saying, "hmmm…106 pounds—this student must be very good in social studies." When the shocked parent alleges that the instrument being used had nothing to do with the social studies knowledge of the student, the teacher supported by a gaggle of salesman, specialists, and administrators in the "Department of Scales" at the school district, might emphatically retort "but this scale is very reliable—we have tested it and the consistency is 99.9%!"

Although these examples may be absurd, the principle is the same. Often conclusions—regarding admissions into special programs, certification of competency, and (perhaps most importantly) first impressions of teachers—are based on instruments having about as much to do with intellectual ability as would a measure of the student's weight. The statistics (which cause the eyes of parents and teachers alike to glaze over, and are frequently associated with multiple choice tests) almost invariably concentrate on the issue of reliability, but reliability is not enough.

■ Validity—Are We Telling the Truth With Assessment Results?

Validity means we are testing what we think we are testing.[8] In some cases, we can create measures that precisely reflect what we expect. To continue the example of the doctor's scale, if we want to know how much a patient weighs, we can express that in pounds or kilograms. But if we want to know whether or not a patient is obese, then we must use the measurement

---

8. Academicians have developed a number of other labels to complicate this issue including ecological validity, construct validity, consequential validity, and so forth. Those issues are beyond the scope of this book. Rather, we are focusing on the classic definition of validity as a reflection of the intended measure.

from the scale as one of several measurements from which we will draw an inference about obesity. The same is true with regard to blood tests and many other medical procedures. The question being asked is not simply, "What is the white blood cell count?" Rather, the question is, "What does the white blood cell count, along with the results of a number of other measurements, indicate about this patient's general health?"

In the context of education, test results are similar to the white blood cell count—they represent one of many measurements that give the educational physician some insight about the general intellectual health of the student. For example, when a student takes a multiple choice math test, what are the things being measured? Is it really a reflection of the student's mathematical ability? Consider the case of the student who is, by the account of a teacher who has observed the student for many years, a brilliant mathematics student. Unfortunately, this teacher is from Moscow and the student's primary language is Russian. The only alphabet the student has ever studied is Cyrillic. We give the student fifty math story problems all in English, all designed to test whether the student is capable of third grade mathematics. The student achieves a score of 25 percent—not a surprising result when the student was guessing randomly among choices a, b, c, or d. We give the student a test again, because the results of this test are at such variance with what the teacher had claimed about the student's great mathematical ability. This time the student scores a 24 percent. We administer the test yet again, and the student scores a 25 percent.

■ The Refuge of Test Experts: Great Reliability, Lousy Validity

What can we conclude about this test? First, some might conclude that this is a very reliable instrument—it provided consistent results every time the student "stepped on this particular intellectual scale." However, we also know that this was an invalid instrument to test the student's knowledge of mathematical ability. It might have been somewhat more valid if the purpose of the instrument was to test the student's understanding of English or, for that matter, the students ability to guess consistently. The choice of instruments that are reliable but not valid—like the example of the Russian student taking a math story problem test—occurs frequently in American schools.

How would you have designed this test differently in order to make it more valid? First, we might have the questions translated into Russian. This would be a good first step, but perhaps would not fully explain all the story problems. Suppose, for example, a math story problem attempting to identify knowledge of ratios and decimals refers to someone as a "0.333 hitter." That has meaning to the American fifth grade baseball fanatic, but it does not help her Russian counterpart in the least. Our questions that refer to yards and pounds may have meaning to the student in the United States who is used to such concepts, but does not test the mathematical ability of her Latin American counterpart who uses meters and kilograms. In other words, translation is not enough if the questions still contain a cultural context that is alien to the student taking the test.

■ Cultural Bias in Testing and Assessment

Second, we must address the issue of the cultural environment of the question. This includes a detailed analysis of the examples and settings used in the questions. In addition to considering such issues as measurement and the cultural context of the activities being described in the story problems, we must also consider the language involved. The example in Figure 4.1 (College Example, page 38), a recent example from a nationally administered test, helps to illustrate the point. Students were asked to distinguish the difference between hatch and hold. As every student from the Midwest knows, hatch is what chickens do and hold is what one does with a new puppy, a friend, or a loved one. The designer of this test, however, having grown up on the east coast and attending summer camps in which yachting was one of the required activities, expected every child across America to understand that hatch and hold were parts of a sailing vessel.

Is this just political correctness? Whenever the question of cultural bias is raised in test questions, the defenders of the test inevitably respond that reform efforts are simply hyper-sensitive and attempting to be politically correct. If our goal is accurate measurement, rather than political issues, then this is an easy matter to address. The previous examples were clearly not measuring what we intended to measure. It is perhaps a less volatile mixture if we remove the discussion from education and return to medicine. Consider the exchange between the defender of multiple choice tests and his physician (Figure 10.1).

The bottom line of this cartoon is the issue of validity. This is not an issue of politics, but an issue of accuracy and measurement. If we expect to be able to improve the education of children, then we must first have accurate diagnoses of their successes and weaknesses as learners. That will not happen when we rely exclusively on consistent but irrelevant measures.

figure 10.1

Doctor and Patient

I'm afraid I've got bad news, Bob. Your weight is up to 176 pounds. So we have scheduled brain surgery in the morning.

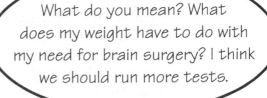

What do you mean? What does my weight have to do with my need for brain surgery? I think we should run more tests.

Well, wait a minute Bob. Who is the doctor here? Besides, I think you are being a little sensitive about this. We've used this scale for a long time for our brain surgery patients, and I don't think we should stop now because a few people like you are going to complain about it.

How Do I Determine If an Assessment Is Valid?

The following steps may be helpful to provide assurance to teachers, parents, and other constituencies that assessments pass the test of validity:

1. Specify the content area to be assessed.

This is easier said than done. Anyone who has undergone the exercise of establishing content standards for academic areas knows that saying, "a student will learn math," means saying little more than "the student will go to school." We can only validly assess an area that has been described with some specificity. It is reasonable to test the content area "describe the issues for and against the ratification of the constitution." It is irrational simply to expect students to "know American history."

The description of content requirements is a complex, arduous, and (inevitably) political task. This is because it requires dissecting a subject into its component parts so that teachers and students can understand what is expected of them. It is inevitably political because it involves making choices. Describing anything as political has assumed the negative connotation of arbitrary and capricious choices, as in "he is being very political." The fact is that we must make choices on a political basis in a democracy. For example, it involves deciding whether or not algebra is a higher priority than band. Because a commitment for all students to learn algebra may require the allocation of resources (including books, teachers, and classroom time) to classes that will provide an opportunity to learn algebra, there may not be enough resources for other things which have traditionally been in the curriculum. This is a political choice because it involves allocating resources based upon the wishes of the majority of voters in the school district. If we do not specify content areas, allocating resources accordingly, then our standards are likely to become relatively dull, useless additions to the library.

2. We must use multiple measures to establish the validity of an assessment.

Let us return to our medical example, in which we are drawing inferences about a patient's condition based on a variety of different tests. We have not announced the diagnosis of cancer, for example, based upon a count of white blood cells alone, but rather based upon a variety of different instruments, including laboratory results, x-rays, magnetic resonance imagery, physical examination, and so on. When many of these methods of assessment provide similar (but not necessarily identical) information, then we can conclude that we have valid instruments. If, on the other hand, four measures provide consistent results, but the fifth measure indicates otherwise, then over the course of time, we may wish to challenge the validity of that fifth measure.

In the context of education, validity can be established by using multiple instruments and methods. Standards-based performance assignments, such as those contained in Part Four of this book, would be a good place to start. In addition, classroom observation, group work, peer observations, independent exercises, and even multiple choice tests (if they are not the only assessment method) can also help to provide the multiple methods of assessment necessary to validly describe the content knowledge a student has demonstrated.

The notion of using multiple assessment methods is a critical one. The greatest danger of the movement towards standards and alternative assessments is that teachers simply replace one set of worksheets with another set. It remains the same drill and kill mentality, and classroom teaching practice has not fundamentally changed. One bad test is replaced with another bad test. Teachers who are committed to documenting the performance of their students must be willing to incorporate a variety of assessment techniques into their ultimate evaluation.

3. Validity can be established by tests administered to random samples of students.

The nature of performance assessments is inherently individualized, yet school districts frequently have a legitimate reason for wanting to assure there is a uniformity of content area, even though there may be a wide diversity of assessment techniques. Rather than invest time and resources on tests for every student in a district, random samples of a standardized instrument can be administered on a district-wide basis. These can help indicate whether the results reported by teachers from their performance assessment are consistent with the results of another instrument.

■ How Do I Check the Reliability of a Performance Assessment?

The statistical formulations for measuring reliability can be quite complex. But at the classroom, building, and district level, there is a more simple measure that can be used to determine reliability. For high-stakes assessments and occasionally for classroom assignments as well, the test of reliability can be accomplished by having two teachers look at the same student's work. They assign a number to the student's assignment based on a scoring guide. If, out of ten student assignments, the teachers agree one hundred percent of the time, then their reliability is one hundred percent. If they agree eighty percent of the time, their reliability is eighty percent, if they agree forty percent of the time, then not only is their reliability strikingly low, but there is a strong indication that either the scoring guide is unclear and ambiguous, or the teachers in question need additional training on the application of the scoring guide to student work. Without question, some of the most frequent criticisms of performance assessments have been their low reliability ratings. This is not an argument in favor of abandoning performance assessments, but rather an argument in favor of clear scoring guides, consistent staff development, and rigorous application of the criteria to students' work.

■ Assessment and Accountability

The hallmark of an effective assessment system is that it is, itself, assessed by the end users—the board of trustees, the public, and other constituencies. Too often, this assessment of assessments has broken down with this type of anecdotal evidence, "Item number 34 is dumb!" rather than a rigorous and systematic evaluation of validity and reliability. Such an examination is rarely conducted on multiple choice tests.

If standards-based performance assessments are to change the way we think about student evaluations, then the advocates of these assessments must be willing to subject them to the same thorough evaluation to which they subject multiple choice tests. This implies performance assessments are living documents that evolve over time, are modified by teachers, and are based on feedback from students, parents, and other constituents. The scoring guides will become more precise; the directions to students will become more clear; the scenarios will become less culturally biased; and the language will become more inclusive. This is not a threshold that, once crossed, allows the advocates of performance assessments to become complacent. It is rather a continuous process of improvement, reflection, collaboration, and yet more improvement.

In short, assessing the assessment is a lot of work. However, if we fail to provide a foundation of validity and reliability for the assessments we create, then everything else in the standards movement will be built upon a foundation of sand. If, on the other hand, this foundation is strong and constantly in the process of becoming stronger, then the advocates of standards-based performance assessments will be able to withstand the inevitable storms that come their way.

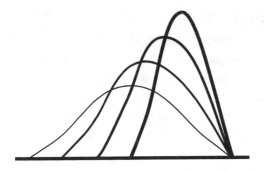

chapter eleven

The Role of National and State Standards

■ The Myth of National Standards

One of the more frequent complaints of the radical right is that the standards movement is an effort to remove local control from the schools. Let us put aside the issue of whether local control is a salutary policy. Consider the Tenth Amendment to the U.S. Constitution, which assigns all unspecified powers to the states. Consider also the two hundred years of tradition in which the local pharmacist, business person, and farmer have much more to say about what happens in a typical classroom than does any national group (including the U.S. Department of Education). Certainly the national government exercises some authority over school districts on areas such as the prohibitions on racial discrimination and the provision of federal funds. On the issues of curriculum, instruction, assessment, and standards, however, the authority of the local school district and the various states remain paramount.

Several groups have attempted to promulgate national standards, but these documents are, in fact, little more than national suggestions. Some of these projects, such as those developed for mathematics, have been exceedingly helpful and have guided much of the standards discussions at both state and local levels. Others, such as the proposed history standards, have become the object of ridicule for opponents of any national educational reform movements. Interestingly, this debate has been focused more on the specific content of these standards than on the fundamental notion of whether or not there should be a national consensus as to what children should learn. As this debate continues, however, the standards established by states and local school districts are the only binding documents that exist in the field.

The United States is almost alone among industrialized countries in failing to adopt national academic content standards. The nations that routinely score higher than the U.S. in national academic assessments have much more organized national educational systems. Many of these nations have assessments and learning expectations that are published at the beginning of each school year in the nation's leading newspapers. Every parent, teacher, and student in the country knows what is expected in terms of academic performance. The national tests, typically administered in the spring, offer few surprises—the content is directly related to these well publicized learning objectives.

■ Our Pseudo-Standards—Textbooks and Teacher Preferences

In the absence of clear national standards, two sources have filled the vacuum—textbooks and teacher preferences. Textbook companies, for all practical purposes, define the curriculum in many schools. Teachers presume that if they have covered the book, then they have also covered the subject. To be sure, some textbooks are excellent, with challenging content, engaging illustrations, clear writing, and many suggested classroom activities that make learning the subject interesting for both teacher and student. The best textbooks also include a multi-disciplinary approach, integrating social studies, language arts, science, and mathematics. Alas, these are the exceptions.

Many textbooks used in the public schools today are beyond dreadful. Teachers who have served on textbook committees will testify to this: texts omit critical skills, are excruciatingly boring, and (in some cases) are blatantly inaccurate and biased. An example would be some history texts in which the biases of the authors are frequently phrased in a declarative manner, as if their attribution of motives to national leaders were journalism rather than opinion. These texts, with all their faults and biases, have become the standard in districts that have not adopted content standards. The presence of this bias in many textbooks leads to one of the great ironies of the standards debate: the right-wing opposition to national standards leads to a vacuum that is then frequently filled by left-wing textbooks.

■ Teacher Preferences—The Standard for Districts Without Standards

The second pseudo-standard is the background, opinions, and preferences of the classroom teacher. To a very large extent, teachers have an extraordinary amount of autonomy with regard to the content and rigor of their classrooms. Thus, some students emerge from the fourth grade with a sound background in mathematics that would meet or exceed most state standards. Other students, whose fourth grade teachers were more comfortable in language arts, emerge from the fourth grade without essential math skills they will need in later grades. Some teachers have frankly admitted to me that they simply "do not like fractions" or "do not like grammar" and, thus, omit those items from their curriculum, or at best, give them only cursory attention. These essentials are frequently replaced with subjects those teachers find interesting, regardless how irrelevant these preferences might be to the learning needs of the students.

One elementary school teacher in a Midwest state devoted three weeks to teaching his class about the internal combustion engine. Certainly there are wonderful opportunities to use the internal workings of an automobile to teach science, math, English, and social studies. And wonderful standards-based assignments could have been developed around this subject. In this case, however, the teacher simply loved working on cars. The students watched, usually somewhat mystified, as the teacher took apart and reassembled an automobile engine, occasionally drawing on the blackboard notations that might as well have been hieroglyphics. No one challenged the teacher about the content of his class—that was the teacher's domain. The teacher was popular with students, parents, and administrators because he maintained a well-disciplined classroom. The students were always average or above average on standardized tests, so the illusion of academic progress was added to this stultifying educational environment.

This example is hardly unique. Instances abound in which scores of hours of precious classroom time have been given over to performances, exhibitions, field trips, and the favorite extra-curricular activities of the teacher—none of which had a remote relationship to the academic content needs of the students.

■ From Anarchy to Balance

Many people fear the implementation of standards will suppress the teaching techniques of creative teachers who have, over the course of many years, developed popular and useful classroom activities. However, standards are not a pedagogical straightjacket. Instead, they create very broad boundaries within which thousands of creative teaching ideas can flourish. Consider the example of the teacher who loved cars. Students could have rotated in small groups to examine parts of the workings of the engine in some detail. In the math/science group, they could have learned about the relationship between air, fuel, and combustion energy, as well as tackled math problems involving acceleration and braking. In the social studies group, the students could have learned about the air pollution control devices attached to cars and what role national legislation played in environmental safety and product liability. In the English group, students (informed by all of their experiences in this project), could have written expository and persuasive essays about the future utility of the automobile and the internal combustion engine.

In the standards-based school, the teacher retains immense autonomy—but not complete autonomy. As in all situations, there are limits. Surely if it is reasonable to ask a teacher not to show an R-rated movie in a classroom, then it is also reasonable to ask the teacher to create assignments which correspond to the district and state standards. One of the most frequent questions I receive from principals and superintendents is, "What do I do with the teacher who just won't implement our standards?" I wonder what the principal would do if a teacher were to engage in other activities that were destructive to children and clearly at odds with district policy. Would these behaviors be regarded as issues of academic freedom?

Would a teacher, even with tenure, be permitted the latitude to conduct a class in a way that was hostile or unavailable to minority students, girls, or students who were ill-prepared by their previous classes? Although persuasion, education, and coaching are all preferred ways of dealing with reluctant teachers, experience tells us that some people will constantly test every leadership decision. If the school board will go into paroxysms of anger over the viewing of an inappropriate movie during a class, then surely a similar amount of indignation should be applied to teachers who refuse to engage in the best practices the district has to offer with respect to standards-based teaching and assessment.

■ Standards as a Filter for the Extraneous

Perhaps the most volatile issue involving standards is the application of standards as a filter for extraneous activities. I am not aware of a single school district in the world with unlimited resources. Virtually every administrator and policymaker with whom I have spoken in the past several years has lamented the need to cut one program or another. Standards can provide a framework in which such resource allocation decisions can be made.

For example, some school districts have academic content standards relating to statistics, and yet there is not a single statistics class in the math curriculum. The traditional math classes in these schools rarely include the statistics content mentioned in the state and district standards. The same district, however, has dozens of classes in psychology and sociology, and yet there are no standards associated with these subjects. A "knee-jerk" response might be to fire the psychology and sociology teachers and hire more math teachers. But a more reflective response might be for an administrator to say this:

> There is no such thing as a class in this district that does not help students meet our academic content standards. But that does not mean we will stop teaching psychology and sociology. Rather, we are going to teach these subjects in such a way that every one of these classes includes several of our academic content areas. In our psychology classes, students are going to learn about the design of psychology experiments and the analysis of their results. Consequently, this class will help our students achieve our standards in statistics. In our sociology classes, students will analyze demographic trends and their influence on our population. This will help students learn about statistics and will help them achieve many of our social studies standards as well. The more different ways we can find to teach students in a standards-based manner, the better prepared our students will be to demonstrate proficiency in all of our standards.

When standards are seen less as a limitation and more as the external boundaries of a very large and creative environment for teaching and learning, then schools can preserve and encourage the creative energies of teachers. At the same time, these schools can insist on relevance and meaning for every hour in the classroom and every class in the curriculum.

PART TWO

Making

Standards

Work in the

Classroom

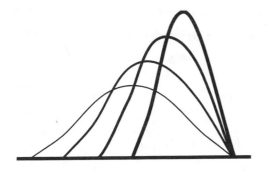

chapter twelve

Collaboration: The Key to Effective Staff Development

■ Alternative Models of Staff Development

The "Dr. Fox" Model

There are three prevailing models of staff development. The first of these is the Dr. Fox Model, named for a famous series of experiments in educational evaluation studies.[9] A gentlemen was introduced to the medical students before him as "Dr. Fox," an eminent expert in his field. His entertaining presentation was utterly without substance, yet garnered significantly better evaluations than did those hapless presenters who offered substance without entertainment. Most teachers would agree this is the most common staff development model in American schools today. Despite pleas that "we don't need to be entertained," and "we want to be treated as professionals," presentations that offer a subtle mix of the vapid with the humorous, all covered with a heavy dose of patronizing sympathy, seem to be the order of the day in many districts. Administrators seem surprised when their formidable investments in staff development fail to show results in changed classroom practice.

---

9. Naftulin, D.H., Ware, J. E., & Donnelly, F. A. (1973). The Doctor Fox lecture: A paradigm of educational seduction. *Journal of Medical Education, 48,* 630-635.

The "Tai Chi Disco" Model

The second type of staff development model I shall label the Tai Chi Disco model. At sunrise throughout China, hundreds of people gather in the parks and other public places to go through a series of exercises, collectively known as Tai Chi (formally known as Taijiquan). The exercises involve slow, graceful movements promoting flexibility, coordination, and strength. Even though it may take place in a public setting with hundreds of other people engaging in very similar movements, it is clear to the careful observer that this is an individual exercise. In modern China, however, many young people (accompanied by quite a few Westerners) have attempted to "improve" Tai Chi by engaging in movements to the thumping beat of disco music, transforming the graceful and individualistic movements of their ancestors into lock step bump-and-grind. Every participant, regardless of individual background, physical capacity, or personal preferences, engages in the same movements to the same music at precisely the same time.

In the Tai Chi Disco model of staff development, the new idea of the day is presented by someone who carries the aura of a Zen Master and presents to true believers the latest version of some insight. I have seen such presentations include comical misquotations of supposed oriental masters, when the correct attribution might have been Shirley MacLaine rather than Lao Tzu. These staff development models focus on adopting a common vocabulary and philosophy, accepting the content of the seminar as the true path of enlightenment. This type of development is particularly divisive, creating a chasm between those who "get it" and those who do not. Worst of all, the research upon which these charlatans rely is frequently non-existent, and the anecdotes often turn out to be repeated folklore, with a few names and details changed, casually floating from one conference to another.

Both the Dr. Fox and the Tai Chi Disco models of staff development have a common focus: the performer and the immediate feelings of the participants, rather than results of the instruction. Of course, they rarely need to be concerned with results, because the presenters are long gone when the real work of implementing their philosophies of teaching and learning takes place. There is rarely follow up, and hence there is rarely responsibility. The ink is dry on their paychecks long before anyone asks if these educational emperors are wearing any clothes.

■ A Better Way—The Collaborative Model

The third model of staff development is the collaborative model. It is certainly not as neat or nearly as entertaining as the two other models we have discussed, but it is the only model offering the opportunity for sustainable systemic change in a school district. There are four distinct characteristics of the collaborative model: First, this model depends to a much smaller degree, on the "guru" whose transient presence is the hallmark of the other two methods, and to a much larger degree on teachers teaching teachers. When outside assistance is engaged, it is not for the "one-shot dog and pony show," but to further a continuous and integrated curriculum focused on the needs of the district. The advent of interactive video communications technology has made national experts available at an economical price for many school districts. For less than the cost of a single day of the entertaining but vacuous Dr. Fox, a district can offer an in-depth, integrated, year-long professional development curriculum.

Second, the collaborative model depends upon context. Consider the model Staff Development Curriculum for standards implementation in Figures 6.1-6.2 (pages 52-55). The collaborative model entails not a single idea or skill, but rather an integrated curriculum designed to implement a comprehensive strategy for the district. This curriculum acknowledges that in order for discussions about standards-based performance assessments to make sense, participants must first have an understanding of the educational rationale for standards. Moreover, an understanding of issues such as cultural bias in testing, validity, and reliability are essential notions in the creation of performance assessments. Providing a quick "workshop on performance assessment" without these essential foundations, is as productive as teaching students about multivariate statistics before they can complete number operations— perhaps an interesting way to spend an afternoon, but not very realistic.

The third distinguishing feature of the collaborative model of staff development is attention to individual needs. Unlike the Tai Chi Disco model, every person is not marched into a room to listen to the same information, without regard to their professional background and personal objectives. This is particularly important for districts that have effectively used pilot programs (please see Chapter 8). In addition, many teachers and administrators already have a firm grounding in standards and performance assessment practices and can proceed directly to the enrichment portions of the curriculum. This not only conveys professional respect where it is due, but also makes the most economical use of scarce staff development resources.

The fourth and final characteristic of the collaborative model is a staff development system that is, like the standards, distinctively owned by the district. While there is certainly inspiration and information from outside sources (such as state and national standards), as well as researchers and teachers who are familiar with standards and performance assessments, the sustainability of collaborative staff development does not depend upon these outside sources.

It is difficult for most districts to break the Dr. Fox habit. It is fun and, after all, we all need a break now and then. But when schools are confronted with the need to conserve every resource and implement standards in the most effective manner possible, there is no alternative but for a profound change in the manner in which we approach professional development. Only the collaborative model offers hope of sustainable reform.

Educators are understanably weary of theoretical justifications for education reform. "Sounds great," they reply, "but what do I do on Tuesday morning?" This demand for practical asnwers to the challenges of standards-based assessments is the foundation for Part II of this book.

The "Ten Steps" that follow begin with a recognition of the most common challenge issued by teachers—"Where will I find the time?" The fundamental premise of this book is that standards-based education and assessment is different—not simply another layer to add to an already over-burdened day. The remaining nine steps include an emphasis on creativity, collboration, and rigor. Together, these steps offer a practical framework for making standards work in the classroom.

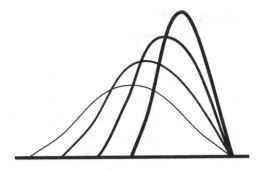

chapter thirteen

Step One: Pull the Weeds Before Planting the Flowers

■ The Toughest Job

Few people would argue with the proposition that teaching is one of the most difficult jobs in the world—particularly when time, energy, and emotion are invested to do it well. Teachers with whom I come in contact on a daily basis are not only exhausted, but overwhelmed. Those who have significant experience in the profession frequently remark about the changes in their responsibilities in recent years. They are not only teacher, counselor, confidant, social worker, and surrogate parent, but they are also the most significant adult in the lives of far too many of their students.

■ Drowning in New Initiatives

In addition to the changing nature of students and their home environments, teachers must cope with increasing levels of administrative burdens. Every year brings "new" initiatives, many of which sound good in staff development conferences and faculty meetings, but are advocated by people who have not set foot in a classroom in the past 20 years. Indeed, many teachers react to standards and standards-based performance assessment in the same way—one more administrative requirement that does not help them accomplish their daily job. "It just means more paperwork, more hassle, more hoops, but not any more support." This is a typical conclusion reached by many exhausted teachers who are confronted with standards or any other new educational initiative.

■ "Is Everything I've Been Doing Wrong?"

With a sense of weariness comes a certain level of defensiveness. "I've been doing this for 28 years, and now you are going to tell me that I've been doing it all wrong?" Teachers have assembled their lesson plans, carefully cultivated over the course of years, perhaps decades, and they cannot lightly toss these aside. Tests that were passionately defended for a generation are not easily replaced by new assessment techniques. Indeed, the very notion that there are any weeds at all in teaching practice may be offensive to some veteran educators.

Nevertheless, we must confront the fact that, despite the hectic pace of teachers' lives and the harried atmosphere of many classrooms, there are some unimportant, non-contributory, irrelevant, and potentially harmful activities taking place in classrooms. These activities must be stopped or significantly changed. This chapter addresses how to identify the weeds and how to prepare the soil for planting a bountiful garden.

■ Standards and Daily Practice

One of the most thought-provoking exercises for a teacher to consider is a careful comparison of every activity in a single day of teaching to the academic standards of the school, district, or state. Dozens of worksheets bearing the imprimatur of national textbook companies have been used for eons and are a permanent fixture in many classrooms. These worksheets fill the weekly parent packet, keep the students busy, and appear to be related to the subjects about which the students are learning. Whether or not these worksheets are weeds or flowers, however, depends not upon their subject matter, but upon the intellectual skills to which they contribute.

Consider this example: A district language arts standard says, "Students must construct a complete sentence, using proper tense and verb forms." Although the standard is explicitly about sentence construction, does this mean that, on a worksheet, spelling, grammar, context, and meaning are unimportant? Of course not. Some teachers, fixated on the matter of sentence construction, limit their evaluation of student work to a consideration of a subject and verb. This occurs even more frequently when in evaluating a mathematics answer, teachers will announce that "spelling doesn't count." In fact, assignments should require that students consistently meet all standards, even if the primary purpose of the assignment is only a single academic discipline. Provided that students have the opportunity to revise and improve their work—one of the hallmarks of effective standards-based assignments—then spelling always counts, as does every other academic standard.

The narrow focus on isolated skills rather than academic standards has led to some terrible teaching practices. For example, honors English classes in some middle schools require students to complete reams of worksheets but never have them write paragraphs or essays. Science and math classes in high schools accept lab reports and story problem explanations devoid of the most rudimentary components of grammar and punctuation. Social studies classes accept graphical representations of population data that do not make mathematical sense because "this isn't a math class." When teachers are challenged about these practices, they frequently respond that they do not have the time to deal with all subjects and thus can only focus on one thing at a time. This is true, I suppose, in the same sense that a person who is drowning in shark-infested waters refuses to take a safety rope because he is too busy treading water and fighting sharks.

■ Break Out of the "Drill and Kill" Trap

The only means of escape for teachers and students who are drowning in irrelevant and meaningless assignments is to have an objective means of applying standards to every piece of work in the class. Because the sheer volume of paperwork can be overwhelming, it is usually appropriate to begin with just a single day's work. Consider homework assignments, classroom activities, worksheets, and every other instructional device for a single day. Ask the question, "To what standard and benchmark does this activity relate?" One of two things can be true. Either the assignment is clearly related to a content standard and allows a student to demonstrate proficiency in one or more standards, or it does not. In the latter case, it is possible that there is a grave deficiency in the standards, in which case the standards themselves should be modified so that this important and necessary assignment will, in the future, be clearly related to the content standards. But if the standards have been carefully designed, then it is likely that the activity that is not related to academic content standards is a weed. It may be a beautiful weed and one that has been around for so long that people have become used to it. But it is still a weed.

■ Fewer Assignments, Richer in Content

Once the weeds are pulled, teachers will find that they can offer fewer assignments, each one of which is richer in content. Rather than a ream of paper consumed with grammar drills, a student can bring home an essay—revised three or four times—that displays flawless grammar, spelling, and punctuation. The content of the essay might include reinforcement of ideas learned in literature, social studies, math, or science class. The parent packet might not be as thick, but the level of student understanding and achievement will be considerably higher as the daily activities of the classroom consistently correspond to the academic standards of the district.

■ Weeding the Garden

Management consultant Art Waskey encourages people to begin purging their work space with a plastic bag and a box of tissue. The former is used to throw away the piles of papers that have been gathering dust in file cabinets, desk corners, and book cases for years. The latter is used to wipe away the tears engendered by separation anxiety associated with losing these valued but useless materials. The same approach might be appropriate for pulling the weeds in classroom activities. The most effective teachers are constantly renewing their professional knowledge, their classroom practice, and their classroom activities. They use their experience as a springboard for future growth rather than a defense mechanism for avoiding anything new.

Once the psychological hurdle has been cleared, and the commitment has been made to pull a few weeds, the question becomes "Where do I begin?" As with cleaning out an old basement or Fibber McGee's closet, the process can seem overwhelming and even dangerous. It is unreasonable to expect a teacher to make a transformation to standards-based instruction in a single year. It must rather be approached in bite-sized pieces. The key to success is doing this in small, measurable portions. The careful gardener will systematically clear the weeds from one square of the garden at a time and will not frantically jump between the radishes and petunias. The teacher who is transforming a class to one based on standards must make a similar deliberate and thoughtful approach.

■ Assignments Grow in Complexity and Content

An important phenomenon associated with the transformation of a classroom to standards-based instruction is that the vast quantity of individual worksheets associated with incremental instruction is replaced with a smaller number of more complex assignments. These assignments are richer in content, cover several disciplines, and provide a variety of opportunities for basic instruction and educational enrichment. In my view, the best of these assignments are created by teachers. (It is important to note that the examples of standards-based performance assignments and assessments included in Part Four of this book are merely designed to be models for your own creative thought.)

One of the most insidious results of the many half-hearted attempts to implement standards, is the distribution of massive workbooks labeled "standards-based assignments" which teachers use in the classroom because, after all, these documents bear the word "standards-based." This is silly. It simply replaces little worksheets with big worksheets, but it does not fundamentally transform a classroom to standards-based instruction. It is somewhat like the teacher who was required to change from a traditional class schedule to a block schedule, theoretically giving the teacher more concentrated time for detailed and complex classroom activities. Upon hearing of this schedule change the teacher said, "Good—now we can show the whole movie rather than spreading it out over two days." The classroom activities did not change—only the format did. If we truly pull the weeds and plant the flowers, then instruction must be fundamentally different.

■ The Hallmarks of a Standards-Based Classroom

As you make the transition to standards, ask yourself these questions:

- Are assignments a "one-shot" affair, or do students have the opportunity to continuously revise and improve their work over the course of several days?

- Are assignments rich in detail and complex in achievement, requiring several days to complete?

- Do assignments dwell on a single set of knowledge in an individual subject, or do they integrate cumulative knowledge on a subject with several other academic disciplines?

- When I evaluate student work, am I only considering a particular subject, or am I demanding student proficiency in every academic subject?

- Is the purpose of this activity to build a skill that will be tested in a different form at the end of the semester, or is the activity an opportunity for a student to demonstrate proficiency so that the assignment itself can become an assessment?

For each of these questions, the contrast between traditional worksheets and standards-based assignments is stark. All of us who have spent time in the classroom will recognize many instances in which our classroom practice has fallen short of the ideals described in these questions. This is the essence of the weeds metaphor. The most meticulous gardeners, with many years of experience, still regularly get down on their hands and knees and pull the weeds. If we are committed to making standards work, then we must be willing to do the same in our classrooms.

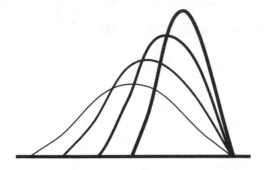

chapter fourteen

Step Two: Identify the Primary Standard

In the creation of standards-based assignments and assessments, it is sometimes too easy to overlook the obvious—that we must begin at the beginning. The identification of a primary standard is a place to begin, but it certainly does not limit the creation of an interesting multi-disciplinary assignment. Rather, it forces the creator of the assignment to address this central question: "If I were to place this completed assignment in a student's portfolio, for which standards would it demonstrate proficiency?" This chapter addresses this first creative step.

■ Where Do I Begin?

A frequent temptation in the creation of any new assignment is to begin with the lowest level standard. Unfortunately, this is a prescription for the "drill and kill" strategy at the heart of most workbooks. The assignment must instead strike a balance between being challenging enough to engage student interest and reasonable enough to allow the student to at least envision its successful completion. Thus a middle school mathematics assignment need not begin, as a textbook might, with the rudiments of reviewing elementary school math. Neither should it begin with the algebra completed at the end of eighth grade. A reasonable rule of thumb is this: At the beginning of the year, start with a standard in the middle range of difficulty. This technique challenges the students who are thoroughly proficient at the beginning of the year, but does not overwhelm students who still need review. This is particularly important for subjects such as mathematics in which knowledge is cumulative. Such a strategy will allow students to continually refine and reinforce their previous skills in that subject. As the year progresses and the class gains proficiency, this middle point can become more advanced. Finally, students not only are demonstrating proficiency in the current year's standards, but they have an opportunity, at the exemplary level, to demonstrate proficiency in content they would not ordinarily learn until years later in school. Therefore, an effective assignment begins with several different benchmarks within one standard.

■ Assignment, Activity, or Assessment?

Readers will notice that the words "assignment," "activity," and "assessment," have been used interchangeably with respect to the creation of standards-based learning activities. This is intentional. Some learning activities can be used to develop student knowledge, performed in a group setting, and accompanied by significant coaching from the teacher. Other similar activities can be used by the teacher as assessments for individual students. From the student's point of view, assessment, learning activities, and assignments are indistinguishable—all are clearly based on standards, require tasks to be performed proficiently, and have explicitly stated expectations for each task. The "test" is neither secret nor withheld until the end of the semester, but is an integral part of the learning activities that have taken place throughout the semester. Each of these assignments, activities, and assessments give the students an opportunity to demonstrate proficiency in meeting a standard or, in the alternative, to make progress toward meeting the standard. In fact, in a standards-based classroom, *assessment is instruction*.

■ Identify Complementary Standards

A major contrast between the standards-based assignment and workbooks is the fact that the standards-based assignment will include a variety of different activities and hence a variety of different standards. For example, students studying geometry will reinforce their knowledge about algebra and arithmetic. Students studying American History may have the opportunity to reinforce their knowledge of government, politics, and geography. Students studying economics, psychology, and other social sciences will have the opportunity to reinforce their knowledge of mathematics and science.

Once the decision is made with respect to the primary standard on which the assignment will focus, then the complementary standards in similar academic areas will begin to suggest themselves. As a rule of thumb, a successful assignment will identify at least two or three complimentary standards in addition to the primary standard. Remember, the fundamental rationale for the replacement of old worksheets with new standards-based performance assignments and assessments is that there will be fewer assignments, but each assignment will be richer in content. This is done not only for the sake of efficiency, but also because multi-disciplinary assignments are more interesting for both teacher and student.

Now that you have selected the primary standard and some complementary standards, you are ready to proceed to Step Three: Develop an Engaging Scenario.

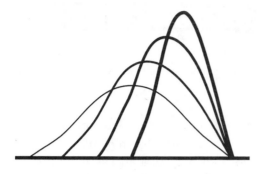

chapter fifteen

Step Three: Develop an Engaging Scenario

Perhaps the most critical element of an effective standards-based performance assessment is the development of an engaging scenario. The opportunities are limitless, and students usually are the best judges of this. Examples of effective scenarios about which students have provided rave reviews include the following:

- Running the Iditarod dog sled race from Anchorage to Nome

- Searching for ocean treasure

- On the case with Sherlock Holmes

- Opening an import-export business

- Is the water safe to drink?

- Competing in the Olympics

■ What Do All of These Scenarios Have in Common?

1. They all allow students to play a role in an adult-level, real-world problem.

It is astounding to listen to students, even in primary grades, express contempt for the way they are treated by parents, teachers, and textbooks. We can smile listening to a third grade student complain, "Who do they think we are—kids?" In fact, students can tell if they are intellectually respected by the role-playing assignments teachers create. When they perceive something as a fairy tale or an inconsequential game, they respond accordingly. On the other hand, when they perceive that they are being taken seriously and much is expected of them, they respond intellectually, emotionally, and behaviorally in an entirely different manner.

This becomes even more important as students grow older. At the secondary school level, it is less effective for children to engage in a mock government than it is for them to identify a public issue and participate in a genuine public policy dialogue. If they wish to investigate issues involving public health, as part of a science and social studies assignment, then they need not "play doctor," but can visit the local health department, measure impurities in real food and water, calculate statistics on real public health issues, and report their findings to real public officials. In brief, engaging scenarios are realistic and respectful.

2. Engaging scenarios require reinforcement of all four core academic standards—language arts, mathematics, science, and social studies.

At the heart of every standards-based performance assessment is the reinforcement of reading and writing standards. Every standards-based performance assignment should create an opportunity for a final written product that has undergone several drafts. Although the primary standard may be selected from social studies, science, or mathematics, the written product should adhere to the writing standards with respect to spelling, grammar, hand-writing, punctuation, clarity, and expression.[10] Although the work product may be done by a group, it is imperative that teachers provide every individual student with the opportunity to express in writing their conclusions about the assignment.

3. Engaging scenarios usually include the arts.

Music, dance, poetry, literature, painting, sculpture, and the other arts can engage student attention in a manner which academic subjects alone cannot. A student who might roll her eyes skyward at the prospect of a mathematics or science assignment, might find such an assignment more engaging if part of her responsibility is to communicate about that

---

10. The multi-disciplinary approach must be used only by teachers with a relatively thick skin. One student, whose faulty grammar and spelling were noted in my comments on his math paper, reacted in his complaint to the principal, "Doesn't this fool [yours truly] know this isn't an English class?"

assignment using one of the visual arts, or if part of her exploration of scientific or mathematical phenomenon falls within the realm of the arts.

Step Eight of this process, Clarify and Enrich the Assignment, refers to the process of taking an assignment originally designed for a primary academic standard and exposing it to the critiques and recommendations of colleagues in other disciplines. Only when art and music teachers have the opportunity to contribute in a meaningful way to math and social studies assignments, will full interdisciplinary integration occur. This is not simply an educational fad or a method of conducting an avant-garde classroom. Instead, it is a mechanism for effective communication with students. Moreover, it is a deliberate means of creating both academic and political constituencies for the arts and other subjects that have typically been regarded as "non-academic," giving them a wide support base when budgets are cut.

In fact, we know that students will learn mathematics better on an interdisciplinary basis. Students who "can't do fractions" can clap complex rhythms including quarter-notes, eighth-notes, triplets, and other fractional relationships to a single beat. Students who "don't get geometry" can recognize the relationships between angles and sides when they are working on two and three dimensional models of buildings. Hence art, music, home economics, metalwork, and other "non-academic" subjects are not frills, but can make essential contributions to the learning of mathematics.

The development of engaging scenarios is at the heart of effective standards-based performance assignments. Before students are attracted to a subject, they are attracted to a role. Moreover, scenarios create an association between academic work and the world of actual employment, and thus students gain skills that can improve business and community perceptions of public education.

4. Students are in a better position to understand any academic concept when they have an opportunity to put this knowledge to use in a real situation.

Invariably we hear that "some subjects are just abstract—you can't teach them in a scenario." I usually meet such a challenge by establishing engaging scenarios on the spot, often with the assistance of students, parents, and teachers in the room. Rather than filling a worksheet with quadratic equations, students can apply their knowledge of quadratics and other algebraic methods to descriptions of the behavior of people, animals, and organizations. Instead of answering multiple choice questions about characters in a Shakespearean play, students can conduct psychological evaluations of those characters, or adapt those characters for a British tourism advertisement. Rather than complete a tedious homework assignment involving ratios, students can identify the challenges faced by an import-export company when it translates currency. While scenarios may not necessarily make every enterprise fun, they certainly can make them more interesting, challenging, and worthwhile.

■ The Role of Parents in Creating Engaging Scenarios

The clarion call for parental involvement in education has met with mixed response from educators. Some welcome any adult assistance they can get in a classroom, while others wonder what contribution non-educators can make to the complex enterprise of working with students.

In fact, some of the things we do, such as the construction of scoring guides and the evaluation of student work, are tasks that may not be appropriate for many non-educators. However, the development of engaging scenarios is something on which parents can provide invaluable assistance. Some of the best scenarios for standards-based assignments and assessments have come from non-educators. These interesting and compelling scenarios come from the real vocational and home experiences of parents. Their contributions are meaningful and can be highlighted in the titles and scenarios of the assignments. But the critical work of translating standards into tasks and describing levels of proficiency for each task remains the province of the teacher. Thus parents make meaningful contributions without supplanting the essential role of the teacher.

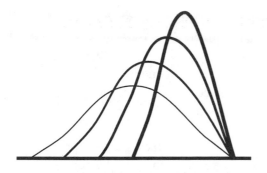

chapter sixteen

Step Four: Develop Requirements for Students to Apply, Analyze, and Demonstrate Knowledge

One of the key distinctions between standards-based performance assessments and traditional tests is an increase in the thinking skills required of the student taking the standards-based assessments. It is the difference, for example, between a teacher education student who is required to respond to a multiple choice question such as, "Who invented Bloom's taxonomy?" and the teacher who is required to create a series of classroom activities that illustrate each level of the taxonomy.

While this example may seem extreme, it makes the point. Far too many answers that pass for "knowledge" in the classroom are, in fact, rather elementary memory games requiring only the lowest levels of thought and analysis. Moreover, the real world of work does not require the regurgitation of facts that are irrelevant to the technological workplace. Instead, the workplace requires the ability to constantly take into account new facts, which emerge in virtually every discipline after a student has completed formal schooling. The most crucial skills a school can impart to students are the abilities to apply and analyze new information with respect to a given situation, not simply the ability to memorize a fixed body of facts.

Most scientists, attorneys, engineers, physicians, and teachers will agree that the developments in their fields since they received their "final" degree are far more important than the information they acquired during their formal schooling. Therefore, the critical part of training is learning how to learn, so that as new information emerges, students are successfully able to apply it to their discipline. Yet, the typical assessments these professionals received in the course of their studies were usually tests that required them to recall a limited set of facts without the use of reference books. In the course of their work, however, they routinely encounter new situations, not contemplated in school, that frequently require the use of reference books. In fact one attorney recently remarked to me that the failure to use references to double check one's recollection of the facts could be regarded as malpractice.

The challenge that standards-based educators face is to avoid "educational malpractice" by creating performance assessments which, as closely as possible, emulate the tasks students will face in the real world. This means that a premium is placed not on rote memorization, but on the ability to apply, analyze, and demonstrate mastery of a subject.

■ The "Core Knowledge" Dilemma

The debate surrounding the need for "core knowledge"—the facts that allow students to create a meaningful frame of reference for their ideas and evaluations—has created a false dichotomy between "knowledge" and "thinking." The proponents of core knowledge include most notably E. D. Hirsch, Jr., the author of such volumes as, *Cultural Literacy, The Schools We Need and Why We Don't Have Them*, and the popular series *What Your First Grader Needs to Know*. Professor Hirsch is quite correct when he asserts that students can't apply, evaluate, and synthesize what they don't know. In other words, facts are an essential part of the equation for higher order thinking skills, and factual knowledge should not be disparaged by teachers. This is reasonable and appropriate—the best standards-based performance assessments require both content knowledge and analysis.

Unfortunately, many partisans on both sides of the core knowledge debate have extended the argument to the point of a false dichotomy. They claim that an emphasis on analysis, evaluation, and synthesis excludes a commitment to core knowledge; and an emphasis on core knowledge excludes a commitment to high order thinking skills. These extreme positions are often espoused when the focus of the debate is the type of assessment that is appropriate for schools. Some core knowledge adherents, including Professor Hirsch, correctly criticize performance assessments that are lacking in rigor and that expect too little of students. Their conclusion, however, that all performance assessments are unacceptable does not logically follow.

■ High Standards Require Both Content Knowledge and Advanced Analysis

Most of the academic content standards of state and districts require an effective combination of content and analysis. It's difficult to talk about the American Civil War in context, for example, if one doesn't know that it occurred between 1861 and 1865. But few content standards would settle for a knowledge of dates, names, and places—students must have the ability to integrate their knowledge of history, literature, economics, and other fields. Academic standards further require that students coherently explain their analyses in written and oral forms. A testing system that required essays but avoided content would be silly; but a testing system, advocated by core knowledge adherents, that relied exclusively on multiple choice items and required facts, but excluded written expression, analysis, and synthesis, would be incomplete and without rigor.

The two sides in the core knowledge debate have many essential views in common: students can succeed academically when presented with high expectations and rigorous challenges. If they can apply these areas of common agreement to educational assessment, students will be better served by their cooperation rather than by their arguments.

◼ Tasks That Require Application of Knowledge: The Key to Effective Assessments

The key element of this requirement is that the student must be able to use the information acquired and apply it to different sets of facts and circumstances. For example, a math student may have learned to calculate the statistical mean, median, and mode. But the requirement for a student to analyze data would take one more step. The assessment would begin with a set of real world data, perhaps the income distribution of several different areas of a city in which only one area will receive income-based government assistance. The student would then not only calculate the statistics, but also explain which measure of central tendency is more meaningful for policy makers.[11] Using written and oral reports, illustrations, and appropriate graphics, the students could make a final recommendation as to which of the neighborhoods should receive the government assistance.

There will be many students who can calculate the arithmetic mean, but who cannot successfully complete this assignment at the proficient or exemplary level the first time. This makes the critical point that *performance assignments are more challenging than traditional assignments. They require more work by the teacher to create and far more work by the student to complete. Nevertheless, students frequently prefer these assignments because they are realistic, engaging, and most importantly, do not involve the "one-shot" terrorism of the traditional test.*

◼ Continuous Improvement of Student Work

When students can take risks, make mistakes, and gain essential information by coaching, they transform their work method from the "one-shot" approach to which we have conditioned students for generations to an approach based on *continuous improvement*. In performance assessments, students have the opportunity to improve their work. This emphasis on continuous improvement is an essential characteristic of the real world of work. Few employees have a promising future in a career when they shove a piece of hastily done

---

11. *Central tendency* is the score of a typical individual in a group. The mean (or average), median, and mode are measures commonly used to report the central tendency of test scores.

work toward their boss and say, "That's my best shot. Take it or leave it!" Yet this is precisely how the prototypical final exam or final paper prepares students to perform. Most employers, by contrast, expect people to work in a team to create a product that will undergo several drafts and, over the course of time, will be edited and improved. The best performance assessments will encourage this process.

■ The Impact of Continuous Improvement on Deadline Planning and Assessment

If we believe in the ethic and realism of continuous improvement, then there are some practical implications for teachers and administrators. First, deadlines for student projects must be moved up to several days prior to the end of a grading period. There must be sufficient time for teachers to provide feedback to students and for students to have the opportunity to improve their work. In fact, teachers should schedule multiple drafts of projects and papers so that students are conditioned to the principle of improvement and the "one-shot" habit is broken.

Secondly, assessments must mirror our expectations of student work. In a few district and state-level writing assessments, students engage in pre-writing activities, including at least one rough draft. In far too many writing assessments, however, states and districts provide a writing prompt and then evaluate the immediate student response. No matter what teachers may say about the value of editing and re-writing, this assessment practice screams to teachers and students this message: *all we want is a one-shot response—editing and rewriting don't really matter when it comes to the test. If you want to teach about editing and rewriting, that's fine, but we're not going to evaluate these skills when it comes time for our assessments.* Students of any age place far more emphasis on the actions than the words of their educational leaders. Assessments must mirror our values about what is important. If continuous improvement is important, it must be part of the assessment process.

■ Tasks That Require Analysis of Knowledge

A major element in designing a successful performance assessment is the understanding that students must apply the knowledge they have acquired. This requirement alone makes performance assessment more challenging, rigorous, and meaningful than the traditional multiple choice test. Yet another significant improvement in the quality of assessment will occur when students are required to analyze the results of their own work.

Consider the example used earlier, in which students not only had to understand the differences between the mean, median, and mode, but they also had to apply that understanding to a realistic scenario. The next step, analysis, requires students to draw inferences about their work. For what sort of distribution is the mean the best measure of central tendency? When is the median a better reflection of the center of a distribution? What are the implications of these inferences when averages are used in public policy, physical science, biology, and education?

Students who can answer these questions have done far more than learn three mathematical terms—they have mastered the concepts behind the terminology. They have done far more than memorize facts. They have demonstrated the ability to apply the information to different contexts, analyze the results, and use their knowledge in the real world situation. This is the result to which educators should aspire for every performance assignment we create.

■ Tasks That Require a Demonstration of Knowledge

Though application and analysis are important, a standards-based performance assessment is not complete without the requirement to demonstrate the results of the work. Demonstrations usually entail both written and oral presentations. If a team is formed to create the demonstration, care should be taken to ensure that all team members have an equal opportunity during the school year to participate in the oral presentations and the physical creation of the written products. Teachers who allow the most gregarious students to dominate the oral presentations do no favors for either the outgoing students or their quieter classmates. All students must master the art of presenting their views in a cogent and persuasive manner.

The classroom environment must offer safety and reassurance to reticent students who, after all, may never have received respect and attention for their ideas. The effective classroom will also convey to the loquacious students that the power of their ideas is not necessarily proportional to their willingness to express them, and that they have much to learn from listening to the students who have usually been unwilling to speak.

Demonstrations also create a living history of performance assessments. They make communication with parents and students about evaluation a much more meaningful enterprise. Instead of attempting to reduce student performance to a letter or number, the teacher is able to show in three dimensions what proficient performance looks like. Research with all ages of children, as well as adult students, indicates that scores on standards-based performance assessments dramatically increase when students are presented with a model of successful performance in addition to a clear scoring guide. The presence of a classroom full of such models makes the proverbial quibbles over the difference between an "A–" and a "B+" quite irrelevant. The standard of proficiency is clear for all to see. Students and their parents can compare their work to the model of proficiency with very little input from the teacher, notice the differences, make appropriate adjustments, and eventually achieve proficiency.

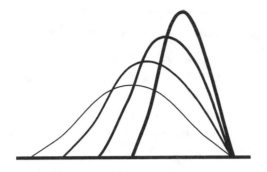

chapter seventeen

Step Five: Develop Scoring Guides (Rubrics)

We should begin with a note about terminology. Some authors have used the term "scoring guide" while others have used the term "rubric" to describe the method of evaluating student performance and its relationship to a standard. While each district may have its own preference when it comes to these terms, I would like to encourage clear and direct use of language wherever possible and to avoid anything that smacks of educational jargon. Hence, this book uses the following definition.

> **Scoring Guide** is a document that describes student performance on a specific task. The descriptions in the scoring guide clearly differentiate levels of performance, such as exemplary, proficient, progressing toward the stand-ard, or not yet meeting the standard. The term "scoring guide" is used interchangeably with the term "rubric" in this book.

■ What Makes a Good Scoring Guide?

In the field of performance assessments, when theory is transformed into practice, one encounters a strikingly difficult task—the development of clear descriptions of proficient student work. Scoring guides not only help the teacher evaluate student work but, properly written, they also help the student know how to achieve and exceed the performance standard. Unfortunately, a number of performance assessments currently in use are not as effective as they could be because the rubrics, or scoring guides, associated with them are unclear.

■ Models of Scoring Guides

The literature surrounding authentic assessment provides two general models of rubrics or scoring guides. In the past, the most common model has been the "holistic" rubric. The sound is appealing, somewhat like a description of a healthy breakfast cereal or exercise regimen. Unfortunately, holistic rubrics have become less useful to classroom teachers as they have grown in size and complexity. In their most extreme forms, they consume a page or more of descriptions. Moreover, their "holistic" nature forces the teacher to apply them to an entire project rather than engaging in smaller mid-course corrections which would encourage incremental improvement. This model is difficult to apply by the teacher and even more difficult for the student to understand. A holistic rating of "2" might be the result of any number of deficiencies, and the language of these rubrics can sometimes be impenetrable for both educators and students.

A better model is the one used in Part Four of this book and in other large-scale performance assessments, such as those of the International Performance Assessment Cooperative. These scoring guides are brief descriptions of student performance for each task within an assessment. Although they can be applied holistically, this model is more effective when it is applied incrementally by students and teachers so that frequent corrections and improvements can be made. Thus, student work can be evaluated on a task-by-task basis by teachers, peers, and students themselves. This makes the final work product submitted to the teacher far more reflective of proficient performance and sends the unambiguous message to the students that they must take responsibility for frequent evaluation, changes, and improvements to their work before submitting it to the teacher.

The following five characteristics of a good scoring guide are also summarized as a reproducible handout in Part Four.

■ Scoring Guides Must Be Specific

An example of an insufficiently specific scoring guide might be, "The paper must be neat, free of grammatical error, and contain all words spelled correctly." These are three different scoring guides, each of which might represent varying performance levels. It is inaccurate and unfair to say, "a student failed to meet standards" if a paper contained two of these three elements, but not the third. But it is also inaccurate to say that a student was proficient, if grammar was flawless but spelling was atrocious. A clearer and more specific scoring guide might include "to achieve a rating of "4," the paper will be completely free of spelling errors; to achieve a rating of "3," the paper will not have more than two spelling errors; to achieve a rating of "2," a paper may have two to four spelling errors; and to achieve a rating of "1," a paper will have five or more spelling errors." A separate scoring guide should deal with grammar, and yet a third scoring guide should deal with neatness. In this way, students clearly understand what is necessary to become proficient in all standards for which they are responsible.

■ Scoring Guides Should Be Expressed in the Student's Own Words

Contrast the scoring guide, "The student will demonstrate mastery in decoding and articulation," to the scoring guide, "To get a 4, I have to read and say all the words in the story." An excellent way to determine if scoring guides are sufficiently clear is to have students express them in their own language. If their interpretations are remarkably different from what the teacher intended, it should be no surprise if student performance is also different from what the teacher had anticipated. The student who wrote, "If I can read the letters, but my words are squished up like a worm, I only get a 2," understands the value of legibility better than the student who thinks that legibility is a mysterious ideal, which rests upon the subjective judgment of the teacher.

■ Scoring Guides Should Be Accompanied by an Exemplary Assignment

Despite our best efforts to express scoring guides clearly, students usually do their best if they have a model of effective and exemplary work. This is not done to provide the students with something to copy, but rather so that students understand visually, as well as a verbally, what constitutes exemplary performance. At the secondary level, the creation of an exemplary assignment is also an excellent way for teachers to think through the clarity of instructions and to refine and improve their own level of content knowledge.

■ Scoring Guides Should Be Created Through Numerous Drafts

Even for experienced teachers, it is an extraordinary rarity when the first draft of a scoring guide is as good as a final draft. The initial draft, when submitted to several colleagues and students, can almost always be improved. If we wish to ask students to engage in the process of continuous improvement by editing and rewriting, then we must be willing to do the same and model that behavior in our professional work.

■ Scoring Guides Must Be Clearly Linked to Standards

Although this should be obvious, it can never be reiterated too frequently. In schools today there are simply too many brilliantly executed assignments based on requirements not even remotely related to standards. The most magnificent charts and graphs constructed by a fifth grade class, for example, do not demonstrate a mastery of proportion and ratio unless they contain an explicit demonstration of that mastery. Colorful maps and pictures of far away places are not related to geography standards unless the project itself contains an explicit demonstration of the accomplishment of specifically identified geography standards. If an assignment cannot be linked to clearly identified academic content standards, then it may be time to reconsider spending classroom time on that activity.

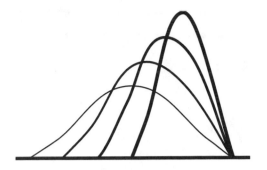

chapter eighteen

Step Six: Create an Exemplary Assessment

Perhaps the most disheartening aspect of many packaged performance assignments and assessments is that teachers and students are left without an understanding of what it means to achieve a rating of "3" or "4." What does a score of "3" or "4" actually look like? Even packages that include examples of responses are not sufficient. The essential process of the teacher-creators developing their own responses is inherently missing in these "canned" presentations. There is simply no substitute for the classroom teacher completing a series of performance tasks.

Although this step is sometimes done with workshop participants kicking and screaming, one thing consistently happens: every teacher responds to the assignment differently. The differences in the exemplary assignments created by teachers produce a startling awareness that there is more than one "right" answer. The addition problem (Figure 4.1) in Chapter 4 illustrates this point.

■ Multiplication to Find Area

Figure 18.1 provides another illustration of this point.

figure 18.1

Multiplication and Diagram to Find Area

The instructions on the assignment seemed clear enough:

The sand box is 5 feet long and 3 feet wide.

What is the area of the sandbox? (Show your work.)

The expected answer was:

5 feet x 3 feet = 15 square feet

One enterprising student drew a picture of the sandbox properly labeled with 5 marks down one side and 3 marks down the other side. The grid was then connected to show 15 squares—15 square feet. Her diagram looked something like this:

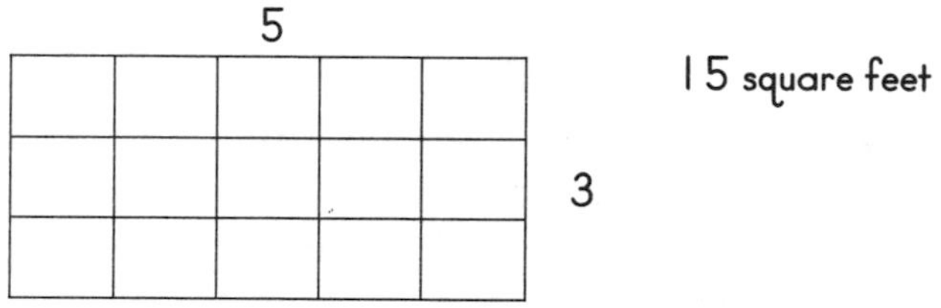

Did this student understand the concept of area? Certainly. Did she arrive at the correct result? Most people would say she did. Did she understand the relationship between linear feet and square feet? Actually, she probably understood this relationship better than her counterpart who simply memorized a formula. What was the grade this student received? A zero—in fact a page full of zeros, because in traditional fashion, the student was required to complete 20 virtually identical story problems. Though she clearly understood the directions and the math underlying this assignment, the student left this particular project convinced that she was a failure as a mathematics student.

If a group of teachers received the same set of directions, I am confident that at least one of them would have responded precisely as the student discussed above did. In this context, the creator of the assignment might have responded with an acknowledgment of creativity and a smile, rather than a failing grade. If such misunderstandings can occur on such a simple assessment, then how much more likely are they to occur on the complex assessments in the later primary grades and in the secondary grades? It is therefore essential that the teachers creating assessments complete the activity on their own and create an exemplary assessment that they are willing to show to students. Over the course of time, they will collect further examples of both proficient and exemplary assessment from students. Too frequently, we have been conditioned that the only right answer is the one found in a teacher's guide or at the back of a book. But the act of the teacher completing the assessment himself is one that cannot be effectively substituted by the provision of a publisher's *Teacher's Guide*.

■ Teacher Content Knowledge

In some districts, the move to higher standards has out-paced the ability of the personnel office to provide certified teachers. In one major metropolitan area, more than 40 percent of the math and science teachers in middle schools are not certified to teach in those areas. Even when teachers are certified, it is possible that the content knowledge required by some performance assessments is different than the background of the teachers. This is particularly true when it comes to the application of technology to an assessment. For those of us who used punch cards for the computer in college, the revolution in the use of technology in the classroom has forced us to learn entirely new skills.

Taking the step of completing the tasks of a performance assessment will force us to learn new skills and to systematically evaluate our own level of proficiency. When such an exercise shows that more content knowledge and training is necessary, it is not a cause for embarrassment, but rather a cause for focusing professional development efforts. In one particularly progressive district, secondary school math teachers acknowledged that to teach more effectively, they needed to increase their own level of math proficiency. These teachers engaged in a three-week summer "math camp" in which they focused on improving their own math skills and knowledge. They understood what too few professional development programs acknowledge—that all the pedagogical techniques in the world are of little value if the teacher doesn't first become a master of the subject matter at hand.

Finally, the completion of the tasks in a performance assessment gives the teacher a realistic assessment of the challenge, interest, boredom, engagement, repetitiveness, or other intangible elements of a performance activity. Rather than criticizing an assessment in the abstract, teachers can say, "I've walked a mile in the shoes of my students, and I understand their frustrations. Now here's how we can fix this ...."

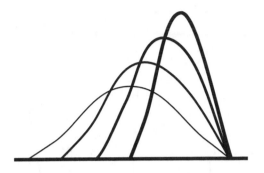

chapter nineteen

Step Seven: Get Feedback

Excellent performance assignments never occur in a vacuum. They are the result of a collaborative process between teacher, students, and colleagues. In order to gain systematic feedback on the creation of standards-based performance assessments, the following are four specific areas of feedback teachers should pursue.

- Student performance

- Student engagement

- Clarity of instructions

- Clarity of evaluation

■ Student Performance

Feedback from student performance is clearly the start of the process of evaluating a performance assessment. When a teacher is asked, "How did the assignment work?" the typical response has to do with an increase in student learning. While this is surely an important outcome of every assessment, it is not the only source of feedback. Moreover, it is important that the estimation of student learning not depend solely on the traditional pre-test/post-test analysis in which a rudimentary instrument demonstrates that students can, in the short term, retain some facts with which they were unfamiliar before a unit was presented. Learning assessment must be based on the ability of students to apply, analyze, and demonstrate the learning they have acquired. (Please see Chapter 16 for elaboration on this point.)

■ Student Engagement

Assessments which are engaging to students, have been given a bad name by those who are firm in the conviction that real learning, perhaps like real medicine, must be unpleasant. If students are enjoying it too much, then clearly something must be amiss. In fact, the consideration of student engagement in a classroom activity is not merely a focus on student enjoyment (although I would hardly apologize for that), but rather it is an acknowledgment that some of the most important learning takes place outside of the classroom. Moreover, if the ultimate purpose of school is to prepare students to become lifelong learners, then it is critically important that they find learning activities worthy of pursuit, even when an authority figure is not insisting that they do so. It must be noted that student engagement does not imply a lack of rigor. On the contrary, students are not engaged by assignments that are easy to the point of being insulting. They are, rather, engaged by assignments that have value, intellectual challenge, and real world application.

Student engagement can be assessed in a number of ways. With older students, anonymous questionnaires are useful. Students should be encouraged to provide regular feedback on the quality and usefulness of a lesson, as well as the sheer fun a learning activity engenders. A large number of research studies have confirmed the validity of such student feedback. A substantial body of research by Professor Herbert Marsh of the University of New South Wales in Sydney, Australia, has demonstrated that student evaluations are closely related to other indicators of educational quality and often are more reliable than evaluations by peers and administrators. Marsh's instrument, the Student Evaluation of Educational Quality (SEEQ), has been administered to more than one million students in the U.S. at various levels in secondary and college classes.[12]

With younger students, teachers may find that students are reluctant to articulate their satisfaction or dissatisfaction with an assignment. Nevertheless, teachers are able to gather very important feedback by observing students in unstructured time. If they choose to continue a learning activity, even when they have the choice of other "fun" activities, the teacher has powerful confirmation that the engagement level of the students is very high.

■ Clarity of Instructions

Colleagues and students are particularly helpful in the evaluation of the clarity of instructions. A delicate balance is necessary here. On one hand, teachers want to be sufficiently clear to ensure that the objectives of the learning activity are met. But the creator of an assignment should avoid being so pedantic that students have no opportunity to respond to the assignment in a different manner. As the examples in the previous chapters illustrate, there may be multiple ways students can respond to instructions and still achieve the learning objectives the teacher had in mind.

---

12. Marsh, H.W. (1984). Students' evaluations of university teaching: Dimensionality, reliability, validity, potential biases, and utility. *Journal of Educational Psychology, 76,* 707-54.

At the very least, the creator of a new assignment should ask one or two colleagues to review it, then ask a couple of students to read the instructions and then explain in their own words what the instructions mean. This process will usually allow the teacher to weed out unclear wording and replace it with more precise language where appropriate.

■ Clarity of Evaluation

The acid test of performance assessments is the extent to which two different evaluators can consider the same piece of student work and arrive at the same conclusion with regard to the essential question, "Does the work meet a specified performance standard?" To assess the clarity of your rubrics, start with the reproducible handout summarized on page 185. Next, apply the rubric to five pieces of actual student work without marking your evaluation on the papers. Then ask a colleague to evaluate the same pieces of student work. If the two of you agree on four out of five ratings, it is a good bet that your scoring guide is clear, consistent, and precise. But if the agreement is any less frequent than four out of five, then some additional clarity is necessary.

Once you have made the language of the scoring guide as clear as possible with the help of a colleague, it is time for the real critics, the students, to help make the assignment the best it can be. Ask the students to rephrase the scoring guide in their own words. Sentences should begin, "To get a 1, I have to …" or "To meet the standard for x, I have to …" These descriptions may be more detailed and, on the surface, less elegant than those created by the teacher. The key criterion, however, is whether or not they are clear and meaningful to the students. If everyone in the class can agree on the relationship between various types of student work and the resulting evaluation, then a huge degree of subjectivity has been removed from the teacher's evaluation of student work.

Finally, a note must be added about the sources of the feedback you seek. These must be people who understand and believe in the concept of standards-based education. Unfortunately, this does not include all of your colleagues and administrators, some of whom are psychologically attached to the old system. A personal example illustrates the point. Some years ago while I was teaching graduate students about assessment, I was criticized by the dean of education for being "too objective." My syllabus outlined a menu of student assignments and specified the standards students were required to achieve in order to be proficient. If the students did not complete an assignment satisfactorily, they were required to submit it again. There was no such thing as a "C–" for poor work—either the assignment met the standards or it did not. This troubled the dean. After all, she reasoned, professors were supposed to be experts, and by definition, were to be subjective in their evaluations, drawing subtle distinctions between "A" and "B" work based on their superior knowledge of the subject matter. When I attempted to explain that rigor should have nothing to do with mystery and subjectivity, the dean replied that if the evaluation system were completely objective, "Then the students would be able to simply identify what they needed to do for an A and then achieve those objectives. There's nothing more to it!"

"Right," I responded, not understanding why there should be anything "more to it." The dean and I were, and remain, galaxies apart in our understanding of the role of a teacher, but the incident gave me a valuable insight into why one cannot assume that everyone agrees with the standards-based approach to education.

Fortunately, the standards movement has suggested alternatives to those who see teachers as Confucian masters and students as helpless pawns. To create an educated populace while retaining a commitment to equity, we must use a process of standards-based assignments and assessments. These assessments must include careful evaluation and feedback, and will allow students and teachers to come to similar conclusions when comparing student work with an objective standard. The achievement of a standard does not require specialized knowledge, but rather should be as clear to the learner as it is to the teacher.

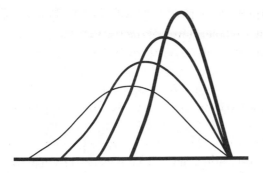

chapter twenty

Step Eight: Clarify and Enrich the Assessment

The feedback you received in Step Seven (Chapter 19) will help the process of clarification. The two key elements to ensure sufficient clarity in a standards-based performance assessment are: (1) directions that students can follow with some consistency, and (2) scoring guides applied by teachers with the same results at least eighty percent of the time. Enrichment of the assessment is limited by the practical problem of time. The use of more complex and interesting activities means that there are, of necessity, fewer assessments in the course of a school year. Thus it is essential that each assessment be as rich as possible in content, covering as many different standards as can be made relevant. Some standards, particularly those involving written and oral expression, will be covered in virtually every assessment.

■ Augmentation for Diverse Abilities

The process of enrichment involves not only a consideration of the inclusion of other standards in the assessment, but also the augmentation of the assessment so that students with a wide range of abilities and backgrounds will find the activity challenging and engaging.

An example of this process is provided in the sample assessment Design the Ideal School (see Appendix A), which originated in a very diverse middle school mathematics class. A third of the students were recent immigrants with minimal English skills and another third had lost an entire year of middle school mathematics instruction due to changes in the school staff.

Thus, in one class there were students who knew trigonometry. There were also those for whom number operations and elementary decimal problems were a significant challenge. In the past, the class had been divided into separate groups, with very little interaction between the "fast" students and the "slow" students. It did not take long for those labeled "slow" to understand that the worse their performance, the lower the expectations were for them. They were, in essence, being rewarded for playing dumb—they earned sympathy, early recess, and minimal work as rewards.

When this class became a standards-based classroom, all students were expected to demonstrate proficiency in number operations and elementary geometry. Those who were ready were expected to have the opportunity to demonstrate proficiency in more advanced subjects. To avoid the insidious "fast" and "slow" grouping with its negative academic and social consequences, the students were randomly divided into groups of three and were asked to create the plans for the Ideal School.

Architectural drawings offer a good illustration of the potential for the enrichment of an assessment because they can begin with problems as simple as the calculation of linear measures and scales—if one square equals three feet, how many squares will be used to represent 30 feet? But on the same problem, and in the same group, students can also calculate the areas of irregular geometric shapes, the angles of roof lines, the weight of materials, and even the load-bearing capacity of walls.

Every student in the group, regardless of his mathematical background, could make a meaningful contribution to the project and learn directly from the others. Because they were all working on the same project and had the same reference point, the mathematical relationships made sense to every member of the group. Moreover, the project was just plain fun. Students designed a luxurious student lounge overlooking major-league-size athletic fields and beautiful tennis courts (all drawn to scale and according to authentic dimensions they found from appropriate reference materials), while teachers and administrators were relegated to tiny rooms in the main building. Each classroom was designed with an abundance of windows, as the school was built around a courtyard and permitted light to enter each classroom from at least two sides. The students went beyond the requirements of the Americans With Disabilities Act (ADA) to provide practical help for a wheelchair-bound classmate. They included creative gym equipment within easy reach, ramps to the copier machine in the library so that all the buttons were accessible, and an elevator to the student lounge and to the athletic field.

■ Extension Beyond the Grade Level

While there remains room for improvement in this assessment (every standards-based performance assessment is a work in progress), the Ideal School assignment illustrates the possibilities of a single enterprise capturing the attention of a very diverse group of students. When I am told, "You just can't have every student working on the same thing when their abilities are so different," my mind turns to the Ideal School assignment and the number of students who, in ten classroom days, learned more math than some of them had in the previous semester.

The opportunities for enrichment are there for every academic field, and the standards provide the key guidelines for this enrichment. A good rule of thumb is that students should have the opportunity to demonstrate proficiency, not only in their grade level, but also beyond it. Hence in a fourth grade classroom, teachers should consider not only the kindergarten through fourth grade standards, but also several fifth through eighth grade standards as well. This is even more important at the high school level, where standards remain appallingly low in many districts. The dropout rate, which many people have attributed to inadequate academic abilities, is in many cases due to the sheer boredom faced by bright and capable students who see little point in devoting three years to a demonstration of the obvious. Secondary schools have a particularly challenging task to create performance assignments that will not only allow students to demonstrate proficiency in high school standards, but will also challenge and engage students who are otherwise bored and disinterested.

■ Engagement Through Realism

Particularly at the secondary school level, the best enrichment is realism. Students need to come to school every day with the conviction that their presence makes a difference, not only to themselves but to others. An enterprising middle school principal in one urban district inherited a terrible attendance problem—students would get off the bus and simply walk away from school. In the afternoon they would wander back to the school grounds, board the bus, and head home to parents who were none the wiser. While some administrators may have hired truant officers, threatened expulsions, or sought other "sticks" to motivate students, this principal was aware of research establishing a positive relationship between the number of team activities and attendance rates. He tripled the number of team activities, starting several groups such as a debate team and sports teams normally available only at the high school level. A concerted effort was made to get every student in the school, not just the traditional athlete, involved in at least one of these activities. Teams were small and relationships were tight. Competitions and appropriate celebrations were held frequently, and students quickly learned that without their attendance, their team was in trouble. As student participation in teams increased, absenteeism decreased. By the end of the first year, truancy had declined an astonishing 35 percent. Why? Students, like most members of the human race, need to be needed. This principal created multiple opportunities for every student in school to feel that their presence was necessary and that their teammates depended on them. These students responded neither to pleas nor threats—they responded to the real need for their presence.

At the high school level, realism need not depend on team competitions, but can include the needs of the neighborhood and community. Students can understand that their participation in a social studies or mathematics class can make a difference in public works, pollution levels, governmental assistance, or any number of areas that can be analyzed in the context of a standards-based performance assessment.

■ Technology

The final means of enrichment available to teachers is the Internet. Students throughout the world are communicating directly with their counterparts in other countries, sharing information, and building bridges. For many students both here and abroad, this may be their only opportunity to change the stereotypes they have held of other cultures. The interdisciplinary possibilities are endless. A few examples include the creation of Internet newspapers (which can be distributed to classes in other countries) or a multi-national dialogue on an issue of public policy, such as the disposal of toxic wastes or international arms sales. These activities include student work in science, math, language, and social studies and present an unlimited degree of complexity and challenge.

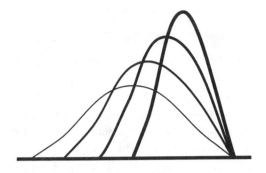

chapter twenty-one

Step Nine: The Acid Test— Student Understanding and Use

At last we are ready to implement the standards-based performance assessment. If this is the first time students have approached such an assignment, it will be as different for them as it is for the teacher. Students who are used to a large number of short, self-contained assignments might be uncomfortable, because for years they have been trained to work quickly and alone, so they can turn their attention to activities they enjoy. The rewards have always been for haste and independence, rather than on revision, improvement, and cooperation. To smooth the transition during your first standards-based assignments, three elements are essential:

- Parental involvement

- Modeling

- Feedback

■ Parental Involvement

Some initial communication with students and parents can be particularly helpful to avoid confrontations. (See Chapter 25, Communicating About Standards With Parents and the Public.) Some students and their parents may challenge the new method of doing things. The parent packet, normally bulging with worksheets, will seem anemic after the first week of standards-based performance assessments. Moreover, many parents are uncomfortable with the idea that their children must work in cooperative groups, particularly if those groups are randomly assigned rather than allowing children to work with their social, academic, and economic peers.

These issues should be addressed directly. Parents can be encouraged to be active participants in the development, improvement, and enrichment of standards-based assignments. Invite parents to school to discuss the assignment. Show them the standards and make it clear how the assignment is built on these learning expectations. Demonstrate how much more challenging the assignment is than the worksheets used in the past. Enlist the help of parents, perhaps by asking them to develop an exemplary assignment or to clarify the scoring guide. While participation by parents is important, educators and policy makers must stand firm on the essentials.

Although the first foray into standards-based assignments may be uncomfortable, the policy must be implemented because it is the right thing to do. It is not only the right thing to do for academically gifted children who need additional challenge and rigor in the classroom, but it is emphatically the right thing to do for children who have traditionally been passed along without any expectation that they can or should meet the same standards other children are expected to meet.

■ Modeling

Step Six (Chapter 18) has already discussed the importance of developing an exemplary assignment. In addition, teachers should take advantage of the resources that are available to vividly demonstrate to students successful standards-based performance assignments. Teachers should also attempt to document each step of this process, including the use of videotapes (another opportunity for parental help). This will help students review their own performance against the scoring guide, provide documentation of proficient and exemplary performances for groups in the future, and also allow the teacher and district to monitor their progress toward standards achievement.

■ Feedback

Because each standards-based assignment is a living document, constantly undergoing revision and improvement, a heavy emphasis should be placed on feedback from students and parents. The feedback must be focused on how the process can be improved. Parents can be particularly helpful with suggestions for scenarios involving their workplaces, personal activities, and community issues. As you shift classroom activities to a greater emphasis on realism, parents, as well as students, will become more interested in the real-world impact of their contributions to the classroom.

You can expect some comments such as, "Why does my child have to work in a group with the dumb kids?" Instead of reacting with anger and defensiveness, it is best to rationally think through the process of learning with the parent. Most parents would agree that there have been times when they have learned a skill best by teaching others, and this is one opportunity created by randomly assigned groups. In addition, you can point out the enrichment opportunities available to students when they have demonstrated complete proficiency in a standard. Most importantly, standards present the opportunity for parents to identify the gap between what their children can do and what they are expected to do. Even the students with years of "A" and "B" grades on report cards will probably fall short on several standards and, thus, cannot afford to become complacent simply because they have been "better" than other students in the same class.

One of the most significant changes in a standards-based classroom is the concept of revision and improvement. Because many of the assignments are done in groups, the notion that the student (and parents) should stay up late the night before a due date to get it finished is simply a thing of the past. Several intermediate evaluations must be provided so that students can check their work against the scoring guide and determine what modifications are required. Parents can also assist the student in understanding the requirements, removing most of the ambiguity, which typically surrounds evaluation.

At the conclusion of the assignment, take some time to celebrate. Ask students to brainstorm ways the assignment can be made more challenging and fun for students in classes that follow. Invite parents and community members to observe the finished products, including the video tapes of some of the oral presentations. Give students the opportunity to express the sense of accomplishment they feel and ask them to write how the project has changed their view of learning and their view of themselves as learners. When the days are long and the profession seems more stressful than you can bear, take a moment to read those student comments. You will be reminded of the reasons why you put the extraordinary and worthwhile effort into becoming a standards-based educator.

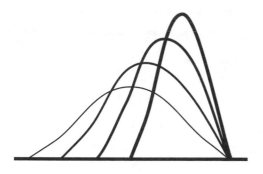

chapter twenty-two

Step Ten: Sharing With Colleagues

If you have faithfully completed the first Nine Steps, you know the development and implementation of standards-based performance assignments is hard work. In fact, it is impossible to do alone, and that is why Step Ten is so important. This step involves taking the time to share the results of your work with colleagues and to learn from their recent experiences in the creation of new performance assignments. Effective schools will do more than encourage teachers to "share your work." They will foster an environment of professional collaboration by ensuring four elements are present:

- Complete documentation

- Intensive and uninterrupted time

- Systematic distribution of information

- A program of recognition and rewards for teachers who create and share standards-based performance assignments

■ Complete Documentation

Although the opportunities for creativity are almost unlimited, there should be some consistency in the format of standards-based performance assignments. In addition, teachers should include the following when creating a complete documentation package to share with their colleagues:

- Standard(s) on which the assignment is based

- Assignment instructions and detailed descriptions

- Scoring guide

- Results of actual student work

- Student comments

- Parent comments

- Personal reflections and suggestions for improvement

The use of this sort of complete documentation package will make it clear that your sharing with colleagues is not a cookbook of how to do performance assessments in three easy steps. Instead, it is a frank acknowledgment that your creative work involved an extraordinary effort and remains a work in progress. You fully expect the assignment to change, improve, and evolve over time.

■ Intensive and Uninterrupted Time

Because school faculties inevitably change from year to year, it is essential that administrators provide more than casual opportunities for the sharing of new performance assignments. A few minutes at a faculty meeting is not enough. Even worse is the practice of copying the documentation list and placing it in the mail boxes of other teachers without a word of explanation. An administrator who is intent on making standards work will provide at least two uninterrupted hours every week for teachers to present, discuss, and improve upon the performance assignments they have created.

Although budgets are tight in virtually every district, clever administrators have found a number of ways to create time for teacher collaboration. Some of these methods include:

1. Media Center Workshops

Most media center coordinators are woefully under-used. These professionals have a number of important skills, well beyond keeping the media center organized, and they have essential information they can readily share with students. The systematic use of media center workshops allows the classroom teachers time for collaboration.

2. Volunteer Monitors for Study Groups

The teacher need not be present during every minute of every class. A number of volunteer sources (including parents, Americorps, Foster Grandparents, Service Corps of Retired Executives (SCORE), and community service groups) can all be tapped to provide a half-day per week of small group supervision.

3. Administrator Classroom Activities

Principals who put their day-timers where their priorities are will spend time in the classroom so teachers can spend time developing and improving standards-based performance assignments. Some administrators spend a full day every week, usually in two-hour blocks, in one or two classes, working on subjects ranging from physical education to science or music. This expenditure of time sends an important message to teachers, parents, students, and central office administrators—standards are important.

■ Systematic Distribution of Information

To ensure information is shared with colleagues, there must be an ethic of consistent distribution of information, including works in progress. I have observed a problem in the early stages of standards implementation: teachers are reluctant to share assignments they have created because these creations are less than perfect. When everyone is reluctant to share work, then months, even years, can pass and nothing happens. Therefore, sharing must be systematic, with all teachers expected to share their results (even for works in progress) on at least a monthly basis. It will soon become clear that these preliminary results have the opportunity to become significant successes as teachers collaborate and work through the Steps in Part Two of this book. It will also become clear if some teachers are unwilling to participate in the standards movement. In this case, administrators will have to make some important decisions about the role these people will play in a standards-based school district.

■ Recognition and Rewards

Teachers who create effective standards-based performance assignments are the real heroes of the standards movement. Their status should be celebrated and recognized on a continuous basis. Examples of effective means of recognition and rewards include the following:

- Publication credit in books of best practices in standards-based education

- Professional development opportunities, including conference presentations and attendance at national and regional conferences

- Cash bonuses for contributions to standards implementation. (Although employment agreements may inhibit some forms of additional payments, districts can purchase the rights to use the creative efforts of a teacher, as they would from private contractors.)

- Publication of success stories in local newspapers and magazines

- Provision of recognition and rewards by business groups. (For example, some local business education committees have provided cash awards and vacation trips for teachers who have created and shared standards-based assignments. These businesses are particularly impressed with the realism, rigor, and high expectations of these assignments.)

Part Two of this book can be almost overwhelming. The Ten Steps to the creation of standards-based performance assignments require an enormous commitment of time, energy, and resources. In addition, they require the willingness of teachers to try new ideas, sometimes abandoning classroom activities that have been used for decades. These new techniques may also require occasional confrontations with parents and political forces opposed to the implementation of standards. The results are worth these efforts because every student, and ultimately the community, will reap enormous benefits as well.

The costs of delay or (worse yet) failure in the implementation of standards can be enormous. These costs are measured in lifetimes of lost opportunities—students who are lost to a system that expects too little in the way of academic performance, and demands too much in the way of mindless conformity. The ultimate costs for society are even greater. However, teachers cannot make standards work in a vacuum.

We now turn our attention to the challenges of administrators and policy-makers who must address standards implementation in district, state, and national schools.

PART THREE

THREE

Making

Standards

Work in the

District

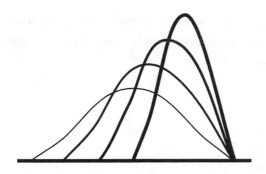

chapter twenty-three

Accountability—The Key to Public Acceptance

Schools at every level must be accountable. Whether it is the one-room private school reporting to the parents who pay the teacher's salary, or the school systems of a nation reporting to political leaders, schools must do more than hold classes and discipline students. In the U. S. and abroad, the dominant theme in discussions by educational policy-makers is accountability. From Nantucket to Nanjing, the questions are the same:

- How do we know if schools are making progress?

- How do we know if our students are learning what they should?

- How do we know if our children can be competitive in the global economy?

- How do we know if the resources we are investing in education are worthwhile?

Test scores have been the traditional response to these questions, but those exams have been less satisfying as a result of both methodological and political problems.[13] Some critics complain that tests lack validity. Others complain that the results appear to be contrived to make all children appear to be "above average," a phenomenon known as the Lake Woebegon Syndrome. As silly as this may sound, it is unfortunately true. In recent reports, all fifty states have claimed to be above average in educational performance. Derived from Garrison

---

13. Hanson, F.A. (1993). *Testing testing: The social consequences of the examined life.* Berkeley: University of California Press. This offers a fascinating historical critique of tests.

Keillor's mythical community in which "all the children are above average,"[14] this phenomenon is a result of the comparison of test scores with a national norming group. This norming group, whose comparison to the national average may be as fictional as Lake Woebegon, creates the benchmark against which districts measure themselves. Hence, all of these districts can claim to be above average.

More troubling to policy-makers is the chasm between many assessments and the academic content for which the schools are theoretically responsible. Academic content standards are complex documents, and it is a rare assessment that can possibly encompass all of the standards. But if accountability is to be reduced to a test score, then which standards are important? Is reading comprehension important, but written expression irrelevant? Is mathematical computation essential, but analysis and application of mathematical ideas unimportant? Any single answer to these questions is inherently unsatisfactory. Therefore, a number of districts are turning away from the use of test scores as they have traditionally been used. This chapter suggests some alternative methods of accountability that school systems may wish to consider as they seek to implement standards.

First, some principles of accountability should be established. Although accountability systems may vary from one district to the next, these four principles ought to have universal application for the standards-based school system:

- The accountability plan must be built on the foundation of standards.

- The accountability measures must reflect both academic achievement and the opportunity to learn.

- Accountability measures must be clearly and immediately communicated.

- Any accountability system must itself be accountable.

■ The Accountability Plan Must Be Built on the Foundation of Standards.

If a board of education wishes to transform the process of standards administration into one more "dead on arrival" bureaucratic initiative, it need only create accountability measures based on the latest political fad, rather than the academic content standards of the district. The only bottom line for a standards-based district is the extent to which students are meeting district standards. Any other measurement is a diversion from this central theme.

In order to accomplish these accountability standards, the district must make a commitment to the technology needed to create a student-based data record. This student-based record

---

14. Garrison Keillor, *A Prairie Home Companion*. (American Public Radio network, 1974). Currently broadcast on Public Radio stations across the country.

includes all of the academic content standards (from kindergarten through high school graduation) and the date the student achieved proficiency in these standards. This record can move with a student from school to school within the district and should be made available to parents at periodic intervals throughout each academic year. The accumulated data will allow district policy-makers to determine the extent to which students (and groups of students) are meeting standards.

The creation of a single student-based data record will also accomplish another important objective most districts have failed to achieve—uniformity in computer hardware and software. In many districts, the computer "system" can best be described as creative anarchy, with students and teachers rigidly adhering to whatever brand name was in vogue years ago when they first learned to use a computer. As a consequence, when students and teachers move from one building to another, they must constantly relearn new software commands, keyboard layouts, and hardware schemes. This archaic connectivity of computers is determined by the least sophisticated machines and the most stubborn building-level computer gurus. Once a determination is made that every building will use a common student-based data record, then everything else—data bases, software, and hardware—will fall into place.

■ The Accountability Measures Must Reflect Both Academic Achievement and the Opportunity to Learn.

Policies that announce an emphasis on math or reading, but provide no changes in curriculum, so that math and reading remain inaccessible to some students, will create only cynicism and distrust. In order to create the opportunity to learn, a school system must acknowledge that the task is not done simply by offering one more section of Algebra I because the school board has decided that more students should study algebra. Creating the opportunity to learn means the district has acknowledged that the academic expectations are fixed, but the time it takes students to achieve those standards will be variable. Hence, it is necessary to offer a curriculum that permits students to take longer than has traditionally been the case to achieve math standards, instead of simply recycling students through the same math classes again and again. More importantly, the school will not tolerate the tracking of students who fail traditional math classes into "alternative" classes that have significantly lower expectations. These classes create the opportunity to fail and are the antithesis of the standards movement.

In addition to changing the curriculum to make it more flexible within the timeframe to achieve standards, the opportunity to learn also means that subjects will be taught in different ways. For example, some teachers are convinced that algebra is an inherently abstract subject that can only be taught abstractly. They are simply wrong. Effective math teachers all across the country are using innovative models, engaging illustrations, and creative approaches to make math interesting and meaningful to students who have failed in traditional classrooms. This is true of every academic discipline. The establishment of standards-based performance assignments with engaging scenarios is at the heart of this movement.

It is important to note that new approaches which students find fascinating do not mean a relaxation of standards. Indeed, the expectations of students in standards-based assignments are invariably higher than they are in typical drill and kill worksheet assignments.

A district shows it has created the opportunity to learn when students can demonstrate mathematics proficiency in their home economics and woodshop classes and when they can demonstrate their statistics proficiency in a psychology class. In other words, the opportunities are widely varied, but the standards and expectations are fixed.

The final element of this part of the accountability system is a systematic tracking of the differences in standards achievement between students of different groups. For example, if Anglo females in high school are doing remarkably better in science than African-American males, then policy-makers should seek to understand the reasons for this gap. It may be due to curriculum opportunities, counseling and referral practices, or expectations established before high school enrollment even began. To reiterate, the goal is not necessarily having all students take the same classes. Indeed, some very persuasive research suggests good reasons for creating opportunities for adolescent female students to take "women only" classes. The goal is for all students to achieve the standards.

■ Accountability Measures Must Be Clearly and Immediately Communicated.

Delays in the dissemination of information spark public distrust about any accountability system, and this prevents administrators from making meaningful data-driven decisions. Once a district has established the student-based data record, within days of every reporting period it should be clear the extent to which standards are being met for every student, classroom, building, and area within a district. This collection of information from the accountability system must be immediately and directly shared with principals, teachers, students, parents, leaders, policy-makers, and other key constituencies.

Accountability, properly done, is not a "gotcha!" by a higher authority, but a strategic tool designed to directly affect the educational environment in the classroom. In creative districts such as Milwaukee, Wisconsin, the goals that principals and site-based decision-making teams establish in their annual "educational plans" are directly related to a district-wide accountability system.

■ Any Accountability System Must Itself Be Accountable.

This means that the validity and reliability of accountability measures cannot be assumed, but must be constantly measured and subjected to challenge, improvement, and revision. This emphatically does not mean that every student must take the identical test in order for the achievement of standards to be demonstrated. Instead, districts should consider the concept of concurrent validity tests, in which teacher-created assessments are the primary determinant of standards achievement, and district-wide assessments are performed to obtain random samples of students. Samples of students can take a district-wide assessment (also based on the same standards), and the results of these assessments can be compared to the data from the standards achievement reports. While some disparities may occur due to differences in the forms of the assessments, the results should be consistent in a very high percentage of cases. If a teacher is reporting that 95 percent of her students are meeting standards, but a district wide assessment performed with a sample of students from that class indicates that only 50 percent of students are meeting standards, then such a disparity should be investigated. However, my experience is that classroom teachers tend to be more rigorous in determining whether or not students meet standards. Teacher-created classroom-level assessments are more likely to indicate a student does not meet the academic content standards than are the results of a standardized test. Traditional assessments might label that student as "average" and hence give him the false sense of security that he is "satisfactory," while the standards-based performance assessment will clearly label student performance as "progressing" or "not meeting standards," even if a comparison to other students might indicate that such work is above average.

The use of this concurrent validity system saves enormous resources for the district. In most cases it will increase public confidence when the district-wide test results show a higher level of achievement than had been reported by the teachers.

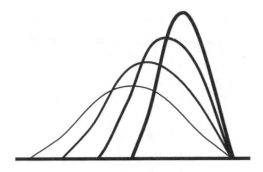

chapter twenty-four

Organizing the District for Standards Implementation

Just as the creation of standards is a team effort, the successful implementation of standards at the district level requires a masterful job of coordination by the superintendent and other educational leaders. It is not enough to issue decrees, pass resolutions, and appoint a standards coordinator in order for a district to become standards-driven. A network of implementing entities must be created and continually fine-tuned to meet the individual needs of the district. To achieve this purpose, I favor the use of task forces instead of committees.

■ Task Forces, Not Committees

The task force, as its name implies, has been assembled by the superintendent for a specific purpose. It is action oriented. Unlike a committee, it does not have perpetual existence. The task force does not exist to hear reports, but to analyze and synthesize information, make recommendations, and take action. The task force exists for the sole purpose of implementing standards and reporting directly to the Superintendent on its successes and challenges. The task force also provides tremendous flexibility. The composition and direction of the task force can be changed at will.

■ Task Force Structure

It is essential that standards task forces not be lost in the bureaucracy. If you expect to attract the best teachers and administrators, as well as busy parents, community activists, business leaders, and students to serve on these bodies, then it must be clear to all concerned that the task forces have clout. In the educational system, that means direct access to and attention from the superintendent. A group of ten to twelve people for each of the three task forces discussed below will provide a large enough group for community representation, but a small enough group so that every individual can make a significant contribution.

■ Operations of the Task Forces

The task forces should meet quarterly. My experience is that a monthly meeting is too great a commitment for many busy people and the absentee rate becomes excessive. By contrast, quarterly meetings offer the promise of fewer meetings that are longer in duration. If all four meetings are scheduled a year in advance (most busy people keep their calendar at least that far in advance), then it will be clear at the time members are recruited whether or not they will be able to attend every meeting. It should be clearly understood that missing more than one meeting will automatically result in the Superintendent appointing a replacement.

Each meeting entails a substantial commitment of time, perhaps as much as four hours. Initially, two hours are devoted to the agenda of the task force, and then another two hours should be devoted to public input. Public participation is essential during the implementation phase of standards. Therefore, task force members must be good listeners as well as people who can articulate their own ideas thoughtfully.

Many administrators have become frustrated with what seems to be an unending discussion of standards. "Can't we just get to it?" they ask. But, as Ruth Mitchell has frequently pointed out, the process of conversation about standards has great merit. Conversation is the heart of community acceptance and support for standards. Moreover, educational systems have a growing dependence on public support, and in the past two decades that support has seriously eroded. A commitment to consistent open public discussions about these issues will go far to rebuild public confidence in education generally and in standards-based education in particular.

Although the needs of each district will vary, and the composition, titles, and missions of task forces can be changed to meet local needs, you may wish to consider the following three key task forces for standards implementation: Standards Development, Assessment, and Curriculum.

1. Standards Development Task Force

The Standards Development Task Force can be the successor panel to the original group that devised your district standards. The principal purpose of this task force is to review, revise, and improve standards. The very existence of such a task force makes it clear the district's standards are a living document, and the district is committed to the principle that standards will change with advances in technology and the needs of the community. The task force should include the most important contributors from the original standards group as well as some new members who are familiar with standards. It is particularly important to include educators and administrators from local colleges and universities on this task force as well as teachers from the pilot project (assuming the district had one) who will have the most direct experience in standards implementation in your district.

2. Assessment Task Force

This group should include teachers who have developed successful standards-based performance assessments as well as parents and business community members. It is essential that the superintendent help to prevent this group from becoming dominated by the assessment bureaucracy that exists in many districts. Although the expertise these people offer in testing and assessment can be useful, they frequently have a vested interest in the pre-standards way of testing. They may even be threatened by the idea that the primary focus of standards-based assessment is on teacher-created instruments rather than nationally standardized multiple choice tests.

This group should scour the district for the best practices in assessment and help to provide the systematic documentation essential to sharing these assessments throughout the district. The business representatives in the group can be of enormous assistance in the continuous improvement of assessments so that they contain realistic scenarios. This group can also serve as the strategic impetus to the district-wide accountability system and mobilize support for the implementation of the student-based record of standards achievement.

3. Curriculum Task Force

The purpose of this task force is to review and monitor school curricula and ensure that every child in every school has the opportunity to meet the district's standards. This can be a very threatening prospect to those who have operated independently in the creation of curricula in individual schools. In the name of site-based decision-making, many districts have dismantled a large part of the curriculum development capabilities of the district, and principals, parents, and teachers have filled the vacuum.

Although site-based decision-making has provided some excellent opportunities for creativity in individual schools, it has also led to some grave omissions from a standards-based curriculum. In my discussions with some principals and teachers about the need to implement a standards-based curriculum, some have responded indignantly, "We have site-based decision-making, so we do our own curriculum." Well, not exactly. When the state and district have established academic content standards, then students must have the opportunity to meet those standards at every school in the district. Site councils notwithstanding, a school does not have the prerogative to decide that it need not offer students an algebra class. Schools have the flexibility to decide how to meet standards, but they do not have the flexibility to decide whether to meet standards.

■ Task Force Results

Each of these task forces should have staff support, including a senior administrator and secretary. The history of education reform is littered with ineffective committees that spoke eloquently about the need to change, while the central office, principals, and teachers proceeded without noticing the existence of those ineffective bodies. Task forces associated with standards implementation must be different. Their composition and operation, as well as the personal involvement of the Superintendent in the recruiting and appointment of members, will signal this striking difference. Some other strategies that will make standards task forces more effective include the following:

1. Public Reporting

At least once each year the task forces should provide a detailed public report to the school board. Particular attention should be paid to the public hearings the task force has held and the emphasis the group has placed on public participation. The performance of the task force on its specific goals for the past year should be reviewed and the goals for the coming year should be announced. There is great power in allowing the task force—not the media department of the school district or the superintendent—to make this report. The news media may be unimpressed with one more unsolicited news release, but they may be willing to cover a press conference held by a major community or business leader who is discussing educational issues.

2. Data Collection and Reporting

Every effective task force must be data-driven. This means that their goals are established in quantitative terms and reported graphically. In particular, the Assessment Task Force should examine far more than the score reports from standardized tests. They must dig into the results of Standards Achievement Reports and other quantitative and qualitative indicators of student performance. This task force should be particularly alert to messages in the data about inequities among different groups of students based on their ethnicity, gender, or socioeconomic status. The data will show whether the "opportunity to learn" is a slogan or a reality.

3. Leadership

Task force leadership should be identified by the superintendent, who ultimately bears the responsibility for implementing standards. The superintendent should not hesitate to replace leaders who cannot or will not achieve the objectives of the task force. Leaders should not necessarily be drawn from the ranks of senior central office administrators. In fact, it would send an important message if one of the task force leaders were a classroom teacher and if another leader was a business or community leader. Standards must be owned by the community, and the role of administrators is to support and implement this jointly held vision.

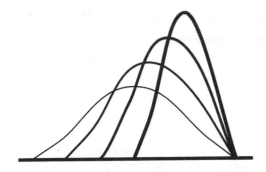

chapter twenty-five

Communicating About Standards With Parents and the Public

■ Defending Performance Assessments Without Being Defensive

In the politically charged atmosphere surrounding most educational discussions, rarely do emotional convictions give way to facts and logic. Certainly this is the case when it comes to debates about standards and performance assessments. The chasm between the two sides of the issue is rendered wider because of the rancorous tone of the rhetoric both sides employ. When the debate should be focused on the issues of rigor, validity, and reliability, it appears all too frequently to be focused instead on an exchange of angry rhetoric.

Defenders of performance-based assessments are "politically correct" or "leftist educational bureaucrats." Defenders of multiple choice tests are, in turn, given such destructive appellations as "Neanderthal bigots" or dismissed as people who just do not understand the problem.

Neither set of labels is particularly constructive for those whose genuine concern is the development of a rational educational assessment system. This chapter seeks to identify some myths both sides have used in this particularly muddled debate in the hope that, regardless of one's predisposition, we can place in the forefront our belief in integrity and intellectual discourse, which are best served by facts rather than myths.

This chapter also offers some observations about the use of a Standards Achievement Report as a means of effectively and consistently communicating to parents and other constituencies about the progress of students in your schools. (The Standards Achievement Report is covered in more detail in Chapter 9.) Finally, this chapter offers some comments about "teaching the test."

■ Myth Number 1: Multiple Choice Tests are Inherently Objective, While Performance Based Tests are Inherently Subjective.

The adherents to this particular myth begin with the premise that there is one true answer to every question. Only an educational assessment specialist or an economist, they joke, could believe that mathematical questions have more than a single answer. Apparently such people are unacquainted with some of the mathematics worksheets common in elementary schools today. (Please see the examples in Chapter 4 and Chapter 18.)

The history of multiple choice testing is replete with predisposition, bias, and outright bigotry. In the 1920s, the precursors to the modern college admission tests were used to demonstrate not only that people with white skin were superior to those with black and brown skin, but also that northern Europeans were superior to southern Europeans.

Clearly, the notion that a limited answer-set conveys the status of objectivity is simply preposterous. The objectivity of a test does not depend on a limited number of responses, but rather upon the extent to which a response to a question fairly, consistently, and accurately indicates the degree of the student's knowledge of a subject. It is possible for a multiple choice test to achieve this standard. It is also possible for a performance-based test to achieve this same standard. Of course, both test formats can also be full of bias and cultural distortion. Educators who have experience working with students of diverse cultural backgrounds, ages, and experiences might argue that it is more likely that a performance based test will be fair, accurate, and complete with regard to the assessment of a student's actual knowledge.

■ Myth Number 2: Multiple Choice Tests are More Rigorous than Performance Based Tests.

This is another popular notion surrounding the frequently fact-free debate about performance assessments. Educators who have administered multiple choice tests know that a certain number of the correct answers are simply the result of random selection. These answers are not even remotely associated with the student's knowledge, but with guessing, rightly termed error, as the word is used by educational measurement specialists. With four or five possible responses in most multiple choice tests, the possibility for random choices being labeled as correct is between 20 percent and 25 percent. Contrast this to a performance based examination in which a student is required to demonstrate mastery of a task, such as an algebraic proof, an elaboration of the causes of the American Civil War, or the dissection of a frog. There is not a 25 percent likelihood that a student will guess right in any of these instances. Indeed, virtually any performance assessment is clearly more rigorous than its multiple choice counterpart.

■ Myth Number 3: Performance Based Tests Yield Inconsistent Results.

As is true of many indictments, there is an element of truth in this. Indeed, performance based tests do yield inconsistent results, but that is true of every single test of any type that has a reliability coefficient of less than 1.00.[15] Multiple choice tests also yield inconsistent results that can be studied and measured. Most of the literature surrounding performance based tests indicates that poor levels of consistency, frequently measured by inter-rater reliability, is a direct function of the amount of training the raters have received.[16] When teachers rely on a two-hour workshop and a cursory review of instructions, they are likely to provide inconsistent ratings to student work. Extensive training, combined with clear and specific rating rules, provides for much higher degrees of consistency. This requirement for clear rating rules not only leads to statistical soundness, but also leads to a greater fairness for the students. After all, they are the ones who have taken the examination. It does not seem to be an excessive requirement for any teacher or any school district to state in simple and clear language exactly what the requirements are for success.

■ Myth Number 4: Performance Based Assessments are Inherently Virtuous.

The exaggerations by the defenders of performance based assessments are just as damaging as the myths of those who attack them. Successful education reform does not depend on the mere implementation of something labeled a "performance assessment," but rather upon excellent, rigorous, valid, and reliable performance assessments. Unfortunately, many school districts and states have fallen into the trap of taking a traditional multiple choice test, adding a quick essay or short answer response to it, and labeling the whole affair a "performance assessment." Such an approach clearly fails the "Duck Test" in which the character of the object of our description depends on its quack, waddle, and feathers, rather than the label we attach to it.

Performance-based assessments, meeting the criteria discussed throughout this book, must be clearly linked to an objective standard. These standards must be described in specific terms

---

15.   A reliability coefficient is a measure of how two judges score the same exam. So a reliability coefficient of 1.00 means they are in complete 100% agreement.

16.   Inter-rater reliability is a term used to describe the relationship of the scores (ratings) among two or more judges (raters). It can be computed in a variety of ways from simple correlation to percentage of agreement. A larger number indicates a greater degree of agreement.

that students, not merely the committees that distribute them, clearly understand. They must also be supported with significant amounts of professional development time and energy, so that the results of the assessments are similar, regardless of which teacher is doing the rating. If students are to be held to higher standards, and this surely is the core of most educational reform efforts, then the assessment of those standards must be the best we can devise.

In making the case for performance based assessments, educators and policy makers alike should focus on the essentials—rigor, validity, and reliability—rather than engage in polemics on the evils of multiple choice testing. Indeed, the political price to be paid for the introduction of performance testing may well be the concurrent use of some multiple choice tests, at least on a random basis. The result that thoughtful people must seek is not a debating victory, but improved educational results for the students to whom we are ultimately accountable.

■ Myth Number 5: Teaching the Test Corrupts the Process of Learning.

Some people believe the practice of teaching the test is inherently limiting. Such a practice, they argue, prevents the exposure of students to a broad range of subjects, and sends the message that acquisition of knowledge is merely for the purpose of achieving the short-range goal of regurgitating information on a test, rather than integrating and synthesizing knowledge over a lifetime.

Other participants in this debate respond with equal vigor that assessment should have a direct impact on curriculum, and that teaching the test is precisely what teachers ought to be doing. If this is limiting, it is only because the test itself is too narrowly constructed or because the teacher has chosen to limit curriculum inappropriately. Such an argument unfortunately, misses the essential point. It is clearly of little ethical or educational value to teach specific answers to specifically anticipated test questions at the exclusion of broad and deep knowledge of an academic subject. However, it can be entirely appropriate to teach to the test when the "test" is not a single assessment, but a year-long series of complex and comprehensive performance assessments. In this context, "teaching to the test" implies a coherent, relevant, and fair series of instructional practices that are clearly linked to assessment. Students are accountable for knowledge and analytical techniques that they have studied. Assessments help students demonstrate proficiency in these areas, and teachers can plan instruction to help promote these areas of proficiency.

■ Teaching Test-Taking Skills

In addition to the essential role of aligning assessment with curriculum, the correct method of "teaching to the test" can help students learn test-taking skills. In every other school endeavor, we expect certain students to learn the "rules of the game." This is evidenced most clearly in physical education classes, in which students must learn the boundaries of the athletic field, the method of passing a soccer ball, football, baseball, or volleyball, and a host of other rules—understanding that will lead to success in that particular endeavor. In the academic classes, students also learn rules of behavior, discourse, written expression, and other domains that will help them achieve success in those arenas as well.

Why, then, should we be at all reluctant to acknowledge that there are "rules of the game" in the common practice of taking tests? Given the increasing propensity in all areas to test employees on a repeated basis, a strong argument can be made that test-taking is a skill, as essential to the successful student as excellent communication, mathematical ability, and other skills upon which there would be common agreement about their essential nature.

What constitutes test-taking skills? Contrary to myth, it is not a result of teachers who teach the test. Test-taking skills, properly developed, have nothing to do with the memorization of specific answers to specific questions, but rather involve the development of mechanisms for analyzing test questions and responding efficiently and effectively to them. The first principle of successful development of test-taking skills is the recognition that it is a skill and not a natural result of innate intellectual ability.

None of us would expect to pass an examination dependent upon our ability to shoot 10 consecutive basketball shots from a free throw line by reading books by Dr. Naismith (the originator of basketball) or attending lectures by Michael Jordan. Instead, the development of this skill depends on picking up the basketball and practicing the skill of shooting free throws. The same principle applies to the development of the skill of test taking. For example, instead of just reading history, students should prepare for a history test by writing responses to possible essay questions, short answer questions, and multiple choice questions.

■ If We Do Not Have Multiple Choice Test Scores, What Do We Report?

Parents and students naturally want to have a straight answer to the question, "how is the student doing?" In the past, this question was answered with a letter or a number. A student with an 81 average or a "C" was presumed to be satisfactory, whether or not that student had met the expectations of teachers and the community at large. On the other hand, some schools have implemented standards, leaving parents and the community with a vague sense of unease. When parents are told only that students are "in progress" on the path toward proficiency, they are left without a clear sense of how the student can improve. One creative response to this dilemma is the (SAR) Standards Achievement Report. (Please see Chapter 9 for more information, including a sample SAR.) By using the same SAR through each continuum of grades (K-4, 5-8, and 9-12), both students and parents have a very clear idea of the areas of strength and weakness months and even years before the threshold years of grades 4, 8, and 12.

Effective communication about standards depends on a discussion that is, above all, committed to the principles of truth and mutual respect. Moreover, when parents, students, and teachers discuss academic performance, effective communication depends on the use of a consistent vocabulary about standards. The SAR is a good first step in initiating these discussions.

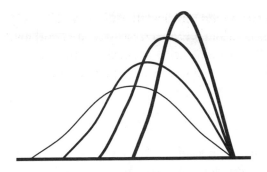

chapter twenty-six

Responding to Constituent Challenges

School superintendents and board of education members live in an environment of almost constant challenge. Political and religious groups, union leaders, business owners, and a host of other administrators and board candidates all believe that they can do the job better. Every initiative, particularly a sweeping one such as standards implementation, provides an opportunity for public criticism. In a democracy, such dissent is an inevitable part of public life. Our fervent wish that political discourse in the closing years of the twentieth century would become a bit more civil does not appear to have much hope of coming to fruition.

Even consultants get to be on the receiving end of this vituperation. I have been excoriated by the religious right for advocating too much national and state involvement in education, criticized by union leaders for encouraging unrealistic expectations of school employees, and chastised by district officials for being insufficiently critical of teachers and principals. If a commitment to the truth entails making all sides equally angry, then these accusations are probably best described as a good day's work.

As most superintendents, policy-makers, consultants, and other educational leaders must admit, we do make mistakes, and make them with a high degree of regularity. Management theorist Tom Peters remarked in a "Skunk Camp" (an intensive workshop for senior managers) I attended a decade ago, that as the pace of society increases in the twenty-first century, we can not count on making fewer mistakes. Rather, Peters concluded, it is necessary that we make our mistakes more quickly and recover from them faster. Effective leaders are willing to follow Martin Luther's dictum to "sin boldly," and there are no doubt elements of this book that fall into that category.

This chapter suggests four fundamental strategies for effective leaders who face inevitable challenges in their quest to make standards work: personal responsibility, focus, networking, and as a final but necessary alternative, confrontation.

■ Personal Responsibility

There are few things more disarming to a critic than simply saying, "You're right—we goofed, and it's my fault." If I had any advice for a superintendent (whether new on the job or a twenty year incumbent) it would be this: the way to establish credibility with parents, students, teachers, board members, and the public is not to try to be perfect—you can't be. Admit to making a colossal mistake and immediately take personal responsibility for it, assuring your stunned critics that they can count on many more mistakes as you move decisively to improve the educational quality of schools in your district. Most leaders will not have to wait too long before making such a grand faux pas, particularly in the complex enterprise of implementing standards. There will be terrible textbooks, bad teachers, inappropriate assignments, invalid assessments, incompetent administrators, and task forces that never get off the ground. Each of these offers the opportunity for the leader to take personal responsibility and, without missing a beat, continue the steady implementation of standards. It will soon become apparent that neither political challenges nor administrative snafus will stop you from your mission. And each admission of personal responsibly will earn grudging respect from those who are used to the administrative tap dance of circumlocution and scape-goating usually accompanying any admission of error.

■ Focus

Just as the effective teacher must pull the weeds before planting the flowers, the leader of a district must also make standards implementation the focus for the next several years. This means that some of the other issues in which the leader may have traditionally played a personal role, must give way. It is not reasonable for the superintendent to become personally involved in budget formation, union negotiations, and capital construction, while they are also creating 25 direct reports and reviewing several hundred performance evaluations every year. Yet this is the norm, not the exception, for the organization of many school districts.

■ Focus Requires Delegation to a Senior Leader

If the leader is to focus on standards implementation—the initiative that can have the greatest long-term impact on the quality of education and the success of the leader's administration—then some of these other issues must be delegated to a capable senior leader. A "senior leader" is not the same as a high-level administrator. The senior leader is a senior executive comparable to a chief operating officer in the corporate sphere. The chief operating officer does not replace the chief executive officer (the superintendent), but instead assumes responsibility for many of the day-to-day issues that formerly consumed large amounts of the superintendent's day. Decisions on school closings, weather delays, discipline, and even a good number of central office staff meetings can be handled by the chief operating officer. Only with this assistance can the district's leader focus on standards. When constituent objections occur the leader can address these objections personally and immediately. If a lack of focus prevents the leader from such a response, then objections can become a public and media issue before the leader has the opportunity to effectively respond.

■ Networking—Cutting Through the Bureaucracy of Complex Organizations

School districts have traditionally been hierarchical organizations. Like most complex entities, they cannot avoid a certain amount of bureaucracy. As anyone who has spent some time in the command center of a large ocean-going vessel knows, it takes an extraordinary amount of time from the captain's orders "right thirty degrees" for the ship to be actually heading on a course that is thirty degrees different from the moment the order was issued.

The decisions of superintendents in a bureaucratic structure can make the ship appear to be a formula-one race car by comparison. In many instances, even emphatic instructions from the superintendent are simply ignored. This rarely happens with deliberate contempt (though that happens in an astonishing number of cases). More commonly the directive is studied, delegated, referred to a committee, and when all else fails, held for further clarification.

Each of these delays provides opportunities for a leader to use a network as an effective supplement to the traditional chain of command. The starting point for this network should be the task forces discussed in Chapter 24. In addition, superintendents can effectively use town meetings held at various schools. This helps to communicate the message about standards and affords an opportunity to hear directly from teachers, students, and parents about how things are going. Even when the participants are the same, the dynamics of communication change markedly when a meeting is not held in the inner sanctum of the central office conference room. Most effective leaders develop an informal network of key constituents. Those who have effective organization and focus also have the time to spend a few minutes every day on telephone calls to cultivate and maintain this network. With an effective network in place, the superintendent is not alone when inevitable challenges to standards arise. Moreover, with a network in place, the standards initiative is not viewed as a creation (and illusion) of a small group of central office administrators.

■ Confrontation

In some cases, the opposition to standards is based on misunderstanding and misinformation. That opposition can be dealt with by effective communication and patient dialog. But there are also times when the differences between the advocates and opponents of standards cannot be dealt with by explanation, persuasion, or compromise. The differences are deep, personal, and sometimes bitter. Examples of these objections include:

- What do you mean "all children can learn." That's a bunch of malarkey—I've been around kids for 30 years, and some of 'em just can't do it. Why can't you just admit that?

- Standards are just another way for the feds to get their hands in education—they are taking away local control and anything to do with standards is simply one more denial of my rights as a parent.

- Standards, schmandards—it's just one more piece of paper on the principal's desk, and I'm doing twelve hours a day of paperwork for the district already.

- Standards are just a politically correct method of bringing every kid down to the lowest common denominator because educational bureaucrats won't admit that some kids are always going to do better than other kids. My kids have always been above average, and you just can't stand the idea that white kids have higher math scores, so you invented standards to prove that everybody's "equal" even when common sense tells you that's hogwash.

I could go on, but you get the idea. These are comments reflecting a fundamentally different value system than that held by the leaders of districts which are committed to standards. However sincerely held, deeply felt, and articulately presented, these comments are emphatically wrong. There are times when leaders need to confront the advocates of such positions and make the case for standards.

When faced with comments such as those above, the effective leader (who already has made many other attempts at communication and persuasion) does not say, "gee Mr. Jones, maybe you have a point there—let's study the matter some more." The effective leader confronts the issue directly. This confrontation does not take place with the oratorical flair of a Daniel Webster or the plaintive plea of a James Stewart. A better model for the delivery of a proper response is Barbara Jordan, the member of Congress who first came to national attention as a member of the House Judiciary Committee during the impeachment hearings of President Nixon. Unlike many of her colleagues, Jordan did not engage in hyperbole or appeals to emotionalism. She spoke in even, measured tones that said, with every syllable, "This is serious business, and these words are not rhetoric but fact." Were Barbara Jordan a school superintendent faced with challenges such as those above, she would have first tried reason and discussion. When that failed, however, I think she would say something like this:

> There are times when both sides of an issue have merit, but this is not one of them. This district has some fundamental beliefs that are bone deep. If this were thirty years ago, and the comment was made that black and white children just can't learn together in the same school, I would not temporize, but I would say that such a comment was wrong and was contrary to my beliefs and the beliefs of this district. That is the case now.
>
> You say "not all children can learn." You are wrong. Our jobs as educators have never been simply to help the students who are the best and brightest, but to reach out to every single child in the school and ensure they

have the chance to prove to themselves they can do things that, a short while ago, they would have sworn they couldn't do.

You say that standards are the result of intrusion from the federal government. You are wrong. These standards were developed by people in our community—your neighbors, colleagues, and friends. The standards are the expectations of our community about what our children should learn.

You say that you have too much to do to implement standards. You are wrong. You have too much to do because you have not defined what the primary focus of your school should be, and standards will help you to do that. If you cannot manage your priorities in order to start implementing standards, then I will find someone who will.

You dismiss the belief that all children can achieve as a "politically correct" idea and suggest that only certain students—usually the white upper class—are the only ones who can really compete. You are wrong. Any district of which I am the leader is committed to the principle that every child can excel, and that those who have done well in the past can do even better. The test scores your children have achieved in the past, or the scores their parents and grandparents achieved, don't cut much ice with me. In fact, we have had too many children with good test scores who cannot meet our standards, but their test scores have confirmed in their mind and yours that they are doing well. I am here to tell you that they are not doing well. If they cannot meet our standards, then they are not satisfactory. And if I were you, I would go home and tell your "above average" child to get busy.

I do not know if a superintendent or board president will ever deliver this speech, but I have dreamed it at least a hundred times. At the dawn of every great educational reform, the discussion eventually moved from conception to reality, and that is when the trouble started. Leaders of standards-driven districts are willing to tolerate a certain amount of this discomfort, and when—after every attempt at conciliation has failed—you deliver your version of this speech, I will be cheering for you.

PART FOUR

Reproducible Handouts

Appendices

Glossary

Bibliography

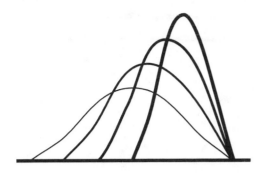

Reproducible Handouts

Comparison
of Assessment Methods

Standards-Based	Norms-Based
1. Standards are fixed.	1. Norms move.
2. Standards are cooperative.	2. Norms are competitive.
3. Standards measure proficiency.	3. Norms (and their counterparts, grades) measure behavior.
4. Standards promote mixed ability grouping.	4. Norms promote segregation of students by ability.
5. Standards are challenging.	5. Norms provide excuses for a "dumbed down" curriculum.
6. Standards are complicated.	6. Norms are simple.
7. Standards address causes, intermediate effects, and achievmenet.	7. Norms reflect only test scores.

Effective Assessments

1. Standards-based assessments are open, not secret.

2. Standards-based assessments are designed so that a large number of students—ideally every student—can achieve proficiency.

3. Standards-based assessments involve a demonstration of proficiency, not a guess on a multiple choice test.

4. Performance assessments recognize the fact that there is not a single "right" answer on a number of test items.

5. Standards-based performance assessments force educators to come to grips with the central question: "What do we expect of our students?"

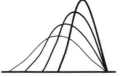

The Role of the Principal

1. Understand the standards.

2. Identify faculty leaders.

3. Create professional development opportunities.

4. Assess student progress.

5. Analyze classroom activity.

6. Recognize outstanding performance.

7. Reflect, revise, and improve.

The Role of the District

1. Ownership—assure broad ownership of standards.

2. Congruence—does the initiative conform with our commitment to standards?

3. Experimentation—develop pilot programs.

4. Support—with time, money, and protection.

5. Focus—consider a one-year moratorium on any new initiatives.

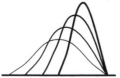

Advantages of Pilot Programs

1. Pilot programs create enthusiasm among the key faculty leaders and principals.

2. Pilot programs allow the initial bugs to be worked out of a system with lower costs of errors.

3. The justification for pilot programs is leverage.

4. Pilot schools provide an ideal long-term source of mentors for student teachers.

5. The use of pilot programs gives the district leadership the opportunity to provide public recognition and rewards for those who are leaders in the standards movement.

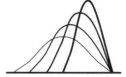

Standards-Based Classroom

1. Are assignments a "one-shot" affair, or do students have the opportunity to continuously revise and improve their work over the course of several days?

2. Are assignments rich in detail and complex in achievement, requiring several days to complete?

3. Do assignments dwell on a single set of knowledge in an individual subject, or do they integrate cumulative knowledge within a subject with several other academic disciplines?

4. When I evaluate student work, am I looking only for a particular subject, or am I demanding proficiency in all the academic subject?

5. Is the purpose of the activity to build a skill that will be tested in a different form at the end of the semester, or is the activity an opportunity for a student to demonstrate proficiency so that the assignment itself can become an assessment?

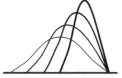

Effective Scoring Guides (Rubrics)

1. Scoring Guides must be specific.

2. Scoring Guides should be expressed in a student's own words.

3. Scoring Guides should be accompanied by an exemplary assignment.

4. Scoring Guides should be created through numerous drafts.

5. Scoring Guides must be clearly linked to standards.

Accountability—The Key to Public Acceptance

1. The accountability plan must be built on the foundation of standards.

2. The accountability measures must reflect both academic achievement and the opportunity to learn.

3. Accountability measures must be clearly and immediately communicated.

4. Any accountability system must itself be accountable.

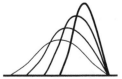

Myths

1. Multiple choice tests are inherently objective, while performance-based tests are inherently subjective.

2. Multiple choice tests are more rigorous than performance-based tests.

3. Performance-based tests yield inconsistent results.

4. Performance-based assessments are inherently virtuous.

5. Teaching the test corrupts the process of learning.

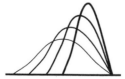

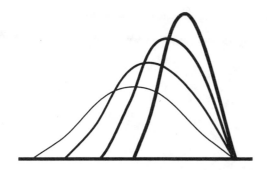

Appendices

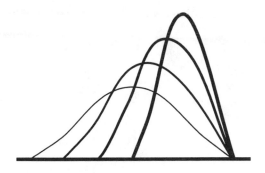

Appendix A

Performance Assessments

The International Performance Assessment System (IPAS)

Improved Accountability Through Cost-Effective, Standards-Based Performance Assessments

▨ The Need

School systems are under increasing demands to be accountable for student performance. Unfortunately, traditional multiple-choice tests fail to reflect student achievement accurately and comprehensively, and many of the new performance assessments are prohibitively expensive. Neither of these alternatives provides timely feedback to students, teachers, and school leaders so that appropriate "mid-course corrections" can be made in teaching and learning strategies.

▨ A New Alternative

The International Performance Assessment System (IPAS) is a set of assessments available for purchase by school systems that are working towards improving accountability and student performance. The purpose is to provide rigorous, multi-disciplinary, high quality, reasonably priced assessments and scoring guides for school systems throughout the world. These schools share a commitment to high academic standards and equity of educational opportunity.

▨ The Commitment

Our fundamental belief in achievement and equity demand that we have assessments that are rigorous, fair, and relevant. Using the best international and domestic models, we create assessments and scoring guides that can become integral parts of the learning process—not part of a week of "test terror" for a tiny fraction of the school year.

▨ The Cost

The cost of recent performance assessments for statewide systems has ranged from $40 to $45 per student. In return for this very substantial investment, schools receive results that are not integrated with instruction, are unrelated to teaching practice, and most importantly, are received too late to provide information for teaching practice, no matter how profound the analysis or how impressive the graphics. The International Performance Assessment System charges a flat rate for each school district, depending on size. This rate provides for complete access to and free reproduction of all performance assessments. Additional services, such as staff development for standards-based performance assessments, are also available at an additional cost.

■ Delivery Commitments

The second edition of the 144 assessments is available now. Delivery can be expected approximately three weeks after the assessments are ordered. Clients receive the assessments in paper and computer disk form so that the assessments can be easily distributed to schools, placed on a district web site, or otherwise shared with teachers and students.

■ Assessment Format

Each assessment contains a minimum of four tasks and the scoring guide (or rubric) for each task. A cover page indicates the academic content standards that are addressed by each assessment. The scoring guides are uniform for all assessments: 4=exemplary; 3=proficient; 2=progressing; 1=not meeting the standard(s).

School districts that purchase IPAS have complete access to the 144 assessments and are able to reproduce the assessments without charge or copyright violation. The assessments include a description of the standards that are being addressed. The assessments you receive will be linked explicitly to your state or district standards. The 144 assessments include 36 for each of four core academic subjects: language arts, math, science, and social studies. Twelve assessments in each subject area are designed to be administered at the elementary, middle school, and high school levels.

■ Contact the Center for Performance Assessment for additional information.

1660 South Albion Street ▪ Suite 1110 ▪ Denver, CO 80222
(303) 504-9312 ▪ 800-THINK-99 (800-844-6599) ▪ Fax: (303) 504-9417
Web Site: www.testdoctor.com ▪ E-mail: perfassess@aol.com

IPAS
Assumptions About Assessment

- Assessments are part of the curriculum: they are tools for reaching proficiency. It is tempting to think of an assessment as a replacement for some other type of test. On the contrary, the IPAS assessments are intended to go along with, support, and reinforce the other things you do to prepare students to become proficient at standards. Educators should use more than one measure to make determinations about student performance. If, however, a student is proficient on an assessment, along with other measures of his or her performance, it is safe to assume that proficiency has been reached for the standard being addressed by the assessment.

- Multiple assessments are the ideal. Performance-based assessments can be an important part of a unit in the curriculum and are an excellent way for the student to self-assess his or her knowledge. In performing the tasks on the assessment, the student works through the material and has a chance to show often and in more than one way that the material has been mastered. Frequent and repeated assessment throughout the school year is recommended.

- Multiple attempts at an assessment are important. The IPAS assessments are designed so that large numbers of students—ideally every student—can achieve proficiency. Multiple tasks and scoring guides on an assessment encourage the use of teacher feedback as the student builds on his or her skills throughout the assessment. Students who do not achieve a proficient score on a task should be encouraged to revise their work and resubmit it, or to redo the task until they reach proficiency. Students who achieve a proficient score the first time around can be challenged to achieve an exemplary score. And those who achieve an exemplary score on the first attempt can be offered enrichment activities.

- IPAS assessments are open, not secret. It is recommended that the assessments and scoring guides be known by and discussed among students. Rather than locking up the assessments until test day, freely distribute them to students, teachers, and parents so that the expectations about performance are clearly understood by all.

- Frequently, there is not a single "right way" to respond to the tasks on the assessments. The scoring guides that accompany each task provide sample criteria for each level of performance. This follows the philosophy that there are myriad ways that a student can show exemplary, proficient, or progressing performance.

- IPAS assessments require the students to "show what they know." Using standards-based performance assessments enables students to demonstrate proficiency when they have truly mastered the subject.

Format for Standards-Based Performance Assessments

1. Title

2. Benchmark Grades

3. Assessment Summary

4. Assessment Keywords

5. Standards Addressed

6. Information for the Teacher
   This section includes the task description for the teacher, any required materials, warm-up activities, and a scoring key for the teacher, if applicable. **Note**: The sample assessments provided in Appendix A are designed specifically for the grade levels indicated on the title page. The assessments are models and are flexible. They can be modified for a variety of grade levels and ability levels within a grade, using benchmarks for the standards. Teachers are also encouraged to incorporate other subject areas into the assessments, especially for students in need of academic enrichment and challenge.

7. Assessment Introduction and Tasks
   These sections are addressed to the student.

8. Scoring Guides
   The levels of performance are described as follows:
   > 4 = Exemplary
   > 3 = Proficient
   > 2 = Progressing
   > 1 = Not meeting the standard(s)

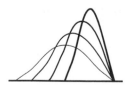

International Performance Assessment System (IPAS)

Sample Language Arts Assessment

Research Makes a Difference

Benchmark Grades: 9-12

Summary:
Students conduct a major research project leading to a significant piece of writing.

Keywords:
Reading skills
Writing skills
Research skills
Oral presentation skills

Language Arts Standards Addressed:

- Students will use writing as a means of exploring thought and as a process involving prewriting activities, drafting, receiving feedback, revising, editing, and post writing activities.

- Students will write for a variety of purposes and diverse audiences.

- Students will write and speak using conventional grammar, sentence structure, punctuation, capitalization, and spelling.

- Students will read to locate, select and make use of relevant information from various media, reference, and technological sources.

Additional Standards Addressed:

Depending on the nature of the research project, it is also likely that students will have the opportunity to demonstrate proficiency in several social studies, math, and science standards as well. Examples of social studies standards that this assessment might meet include the following:

- Students will evaluate competing arguments about the proper role of government in the major areas of domestic and foreign policy.

    - Students will develop proposals regarding solutions to significant political, demographic, or environmental issues.

(continued)

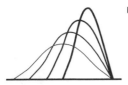

Research Makes a Difference (continued)

Information for the Teacher

■ TASK DESCRIPTION

Students are asked to imagine they are working as an assistant for a policymaker in Washington D.C.

This project requires students to identify a public policy issue, frame a research question, conduct an investigation using research resources, and present both oral and written reports on the results of their research.

Encourage students to use available resources such as photographs, videotapes, and tape-recorded interviews. Poster boards or other visual aids may be used for the oral presentation. We strongly encourage videotaping the oral presentations. This will not only help to create a formal atmosphere for the presentations, but it will also assist you in coaching students for potential presentations before actual policymakers. Videotaping presentations will also help you develop a personal library of exemplary assignments for consideration by future students.

Regular progress reports and reviews are encouraged throughout this assessment. Although it is possible to complete this assignment in three weeks, it will be most successful if this is viewed as a "culminating" activity and the tasks of the assessment are developed over the course of at least two months.

■ REQUIRED MATERIALS

– Information about local experts to interview
– Research materials
– Computers for research and writing (optional)

Assessment Introduction—Here is what you will do...

You have volunteered to work for a local politician who needs your help generating ideas for an upcoming campaign. Because she wants to get in touch with the youth of today, she has asked you to choose a topic that is important in the lives of people your age. You will investigate the topic and present her with an extensive paper based on outstanding research and documentation. She will use this information in an upcoming campaign kick-off speech.

(continued)

Task 1: Selecting a topic

The politician you are working for is a very bright woman who understands the importance of choosing a good topic. Sometimes the challenge in writing a research paper is selecting a topic that is not too broad and not too narrow or limited. Another challenge is making sure that the topic is interesting to **you**, the researcher. It should be something that will make a difference in your life and the lives of other people you care about.

Here is what you will do.

1) Talk with your friends and classmates about what is important to people at your stage in life. Write down ten ideas for a topic. One way to get ideas is to look in a newspaper or newsmagazine for current policy issues. Examples of topics you might find include:

- Music censorship
- Land use issues
- Educational reform
- Drug abuse
- The effect of divorce on teenagers
- Youth violence
- Pollution of local air and water
- Homeless people in your town
- Illiteracy among teens and adults

The list could go on and on, but you get the idea- select a topic that is, above all, important to you and your peers.

2) Review the ten ideas and choose one that sounds particularly interesting to you. Write down your topic and describe why you chose it.

3) Turn this in to your teacher. You must have your teacher approve your choice before you can continue. Your teacher can also be a great source of ideas. He or she may have you revise your topic to help you make the topic more manageable.

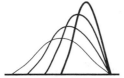

(continued)

Scoring Guide—Task 1

4 Exemplary

- The student discusses important issues with peers and generates at least ten ideas for a research topic.

- From that list, a reasonable topic for research is chosen. The topic is not too broad or too narrow. The topic is clearly stated in writing, along with the reasons why the student would like to research the issue.

- Advanced work is included. For example, the student writes extensively about the importance of the issue and its impact on society. The student provides examples from his or her life or from society that illustrate the need for this research.

3 Proficient

- The student discusses important issues with peers and generates at least ten ideas for a research topic.

- From that list, a reasonable topic for research is chosen. The topic is not too broad or too narrow. The topic is clearly stated in writing, along with the reasons why the student would like to research the issue.

2 Progressing

- The student discusses important issues with peers and generates at least five ideas for a research topic.

- From that list, a topic is chosen. The topic is important, but the issue is vague or unclear. The topic is too broad or too narrow, and would be difficult to research in its present form.

- Revision of the topic is necessary.

1 Not meeting the standard(s)

- A topic is chosen, but it is not clear how the student decided on it or why he or she wants to study it further. The topic is not understandable in its present form.

- The task should be repeated after further instruction.

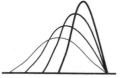

(continued)

Task 2: Decide what resources you will research

When you are beginning a research project, a little bit of planning goes a long way. Before you start your search, decide where to look for useful information about your chosen topic. Consider primary and secondary sources.

- First, make a list of research materials that are related to your topic. The librarian or media center specialist in your school can be a great help here. Start with resources that are easy to find, such as books, magazines, newspapers, and journals. Other good places to look are databases (catalogs of information on the computer) and printed surveys of the literature. Look for articles or books that survey what has been written about your topic. Look for articles and books that have extensive bibliographies. Try to find 15 sources that you will research. If you can find more, go for it.

- Second, make a list of several people you would like to interview about this topic. At least one of these people should be located in your area so you can conduct the interview in person or by phone. Depending on your topic these people could be public officials, instructors at a local college or university, newspaper writers, or other people who have special knowledge about the topic that you want to research. You may be able to phone or write letters to people who are far away, or ask them questions over e-mail.

- Finally, if you have access to a directory of Internet sites, find at least five Internet sites that you might also use in your search for information.

Prepare a documented list of all your sources. Turn this list in to your teacher.

Scoring Guide—Task 2

4 Exemplary

- The student prepares an extensive list of resources. The list includes at least 15 different sources from at least three different types of resources. This is a good first draft of a list that contains most of the documentation the student will need for the reference section of the final paper. The list of potential interview subjects includes each person's full name, address, and telephone number. Each item on the list appears to be clearly related to the topic.

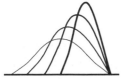

(continued)

■ The student shows advanced research strategies. For example, more than 15 sources are documented. The sources come from a wide range of materials including books, magazines, newspapers, journals, Internet sites, and from several persons to interview. Each item on the list includes complete documentation so that another researcher could easily find the item and so that the items can be accurately listed in the reference section of the final paper. The items cover a wide range of areas related to the topic.

3 Proficient

■ The student prepares an extensive list of resources. The list includes at least 15 different sources from at least three different types of resources. This is an acceptable first draft of a list that contains most of the documentation the student will need for the reference section of the final paper. The list of potential interview subjects includes each person's full name, address, and telephone number. Each item on the list appears to be clearly related to the topic.

2 Progressing

■ The student prepares a list of resources. The list includes at least 10 different sources from at least two different types of resources. The list includes two potential interview subjects, but only names are given.

■ Significant information is missing from the documentation that will be used in the reference section of the final paper. Some of the items on the list do not appear to be related to the topic.

■ The student needs to return to the media center to complete the list.

1 Not meeting the standard(s)

■ The student attempts a list of resources. The list has fewer than 10 sources, is incomplete, or contains sources that are not closely related to the topic. The list cannot support a significant research project.

■ The task should be repeated after additional instruction.

(continued)

Task 3: Read your sources

Start gathering your research. Based on the list you made in Task 2, start reading the documents.

It is important to be carefully organized here. Documenting information on index cards is one effective way to organize your research process. When you find information in one of your documents, write a brief quote on the index card. On the top of each card, write one word or phrase describing the content of that card. You will likely have several cards from one book or magazine. Be sure to include all the information you will need for your reference list—author, title, publisher, date, volume, page, and so on. If you discover additional sources from reading sources on your original list, don't forget to add them to your bibliography.

Turn in the note cards that you have prepared to your teacher.

Scoring Guide—Task 3

4 Exemplary

- The student gathers original resources and reads materials. Additional resources are added to the list.

- Note cards or notes are completed for each piece of information the student uses. Each card or note contains a quotation and all the necessary information needed in the reference list of the paper.

- The student demonstrates advanced research skills. For example, at least 35 research cards, representing at least ten different research sources, are prepared. Every card has a subject title so that the cards can be used to create an outline for the paper.

3 Proficient

- The student gathers original resources and reads materials. Additional resources are added to the list.

- Note cards or notes are completed for each piece of information the student uses, and each card contains a quotation and all the necessary information needed in the reference list of the paper. At least 25 research cards, representing at least eight different research sources, are prepared.

(continued)

2 Progressing

- At least 15 research cards, representing at least five different research sources are presented. The cards are on the right subject, but problems with neatness, complete information, and subject titles make it difficult to use these cards to create an outline.

- The student needs to return to the library to improve the notes before proceeding.

1 Not meeting the standard(s)

- Less than 15 research cards are prepared or the cards are from less than five different research sources. The cards are not clearly related to the research subject. They are not legible, or lack the information necessary to make them useful. The cards cannot support a good research paper.

- The task should be repeated.

Task 4: Interview an expert

By now you are learning a great deal about your subject, but you probably still have some questions that an outside expert could answer. Next, you will conduct an interview.

Decide who you would like to interview. Use your list from Task 2.

- Write a business letter to an expert requesting thirty minutes of their time for an interview for a research project on your subject. Explain what class you are in and mention some of the sources you have read to prepare for the interview.

- Five days after you send the letter, follow up with a telephone call to set an appointment for the interview.

- When the interview appointment is set, write a list of questions for the interview. The best questions are "open-ended" questions – that is, the expert is asked to explain something rather than simply give you a "yes or no" answer. Review the notes you created in Task 3 to help form your questions. You may want to take a tape recorder to the interview. If you do this, you must ask permission before you start tape-recording the interview. Also, ask the expert if he or she can recommend a person or group with whom you can share the results of your research.

- As soon as the interview is over, write a thank you note to the person you interviewed.

(continued)

If it is not possible to find a local person to interview, try using e-mail or arranging a telephone interview.

Turn in your list of questions and the business letter to your teacher. Include a summary of how you attempted to contact the expert and a description of the interview, if it was conducted.

Scoring Guide—Task 4

4 Exemplary

- A business letter is written to an expert asking for the interview. It clearly explains the reasons for the request. The language and style are appropriate for the individual.

- The questions for the interview are relevant and clearly based on the research done in Task 3.

- The letter is sent, and the follow up call is placed. If the person agrees, the interview is conducted. If the person cannot be scheduled for an interview, the process is repeated for a second person.

- A thank you note is sent after the interview.

- The student writes a summary of how the expert was contacted and a description of the interview.

- Additional work is completed. For example, the interview questions are exceptionally well written. The student conducts more than one interview.

3 Proficient

- A business letter is written to an expert asking for the interview. It clearly explains the reasons for the request. The language and style are appropriate for the individual.

- The questions for the interview are relevant and clearly based on the research done in Task 3.

- The letter is sent, and the follow up call is placed. If the person agrees, the interview is conducted. If the person cannot be scheduled for an interview, the process is repeated for a second person.

- A thank you note is sent after the interview.

   - The student writes a summary of how the expert was contacted and a description of the interview.

(continued)

2 Progressing

- The business letter contains errors and must be rewritten.

- The questions are not relevant or clear.

- Additional work is needed.

1 Not meeting the standard(s)

- The business letter contains errors, is unclear, or is incomplete.

- The task should be repeated.

Task 5: Outline your paper

Organize all of the material you have collected in preparation for your paper. With the results of your interview and the other research you have done, you are starting to see the information you have gathered fall into a logical order.

Create an outline for your research paper. Your teacher may have a specific format for you to follow. If not, here is one style many students find useful. Specify which research cards apply to each section.

I.   Introduction
    A.   What is the issue?
    B.   Why is this issue important?
    C.   Who does this issue affect?
II. Background of the Issue
    A.   When did the problem or issue begin?
    B.   How has the issue changed over time?
III. Alternative Solutions or perspectives
    A.   List several different alternatives here.
    B.   For each alternative solution or perspective, discuss advantages and disadvantages.
IV. Recommendations
    Based on the information in Part III, make a recommendation for the best solution to this problem. You can also recommend that additional research is necessary, and include some of the research you discovered in Task 2 but did not have time to personally investigate. This could include possible interviews with experts, Internet sites, and other research resources.
V.   Conclusions
VI. Reference List
VII. Appendices

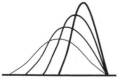

(continued)

Scoring Guide—Task 5

4 Exemplary

- An outline is created using the notes from Tasks 3 and 4.

- The outline follows the format that was given by the teacher. Each point of the outline is supported by research conducted by the student.

- The outline is exceptionally well organized and clear.

3 Proficient

- An outline is created using the notes from Tasks 3 and 4.

- The outline follows the format that was given by the teacher. Each point of the outline is supported by research conducted by the student.

2 Progressing

- The outline is missing some of the elements prescribed by the teacher.

- Many sections are not related to the research conducted by the student.

1 Not meeting the standard(s)

- The outline is not organized or is missing important pieces. It is not related to the research conducted in earlier tasks.

- The task should be repeated.

Task 6: Write the first draft

You are ready to write the first draft of your paper.

Your first draft is one of the most important parts of this entire project. The only way for you to have a good paper is to do a first draft, and then edit and correct it. There are always improvements that can be made. If you are not sure about the form your teacher wants you to use, ask for a copy of a research paper he or she regards as superior.

Prepare the first draft of your paper. Submit it for comments from your teacher and at least one other student. Take all of these comments into account when you create your final paper.

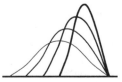

(continued)

Scoring Guide—Task 6

4 Exemplary

- A first draft is written and submitted to the teacher and one other student for review.

- The first draft is flawless in format, grammar, and spelling. It presents the research in an exceptionally clear and organized fashion.

3 Proficient

- A first draft is written and submitted to the teacher and one other student for review.

- Some editing remains in order to improve expression and clarify ideas.

2 Progressing

- A first draft is written and submitted to the teacher and one other student for review.

- The paper does not follow the format prescribed by the teacher or contains major errors in spelling and grammar.

- Another draft must be created and reviewed before proceeding to the final draft stage.

1 Not meeting the standard(s)

- A first draft is written and submitted to the teacher and one other student for review.

- The paper is illegible, does not follow the prescribed format, or contains so many errors in spelling and grammar that it is difficult or impossible to read for content.

- Another draft must be created and reviewed before proceeding to the final draft stage.

Task 7: Write the final paper

Revise you paper based on the comments you received on your first draft. Consider each comment you received and decide how to change you paper to respond to the comment. If your draft is still not as good as it should be, you may need to repeat Task 6.

Submit your final paper to your teacher.

(continued)

Scoring Guide—Task 7

4 Exemplary

- The paper is flawless in format and written expression. It describes the issue well and presents appropriate background of the issue. It presents more than one alternative policy and provides a persuasive, logical, and well-reasoned conclusion that recommends an appropriate course of action. Each claim or quotation is documented using sources that support the conclusion. Footnotes or endnotes use appropriate formats. The paper uses the sources found in the earlier tasks.

- Each claim or quotation is correctly documented using sources that support the conclusion.

- The paper uses the sources found in the earlier tasks.

- Comments from Task 6 are incorporated into the final paper.

3 Proficient

- The paper describes the issue well and presents appropriate background of the issue. It presents at least one alternative policy and provides a persuasive, logical, and well-reasoned conclusion that recommends an appropriate course of action. The paper contains only minor errors in format and written expression.

- Each claim or quotation is documented using sources that support the conclusion.

- The paper uses the sources found in the earlier tasks.

- Comments from Task 6 are incorporated into the final paper.

2 Progressing

- More alternative policies should be discussed and more details should be provided. The conclusion lacks clarity and persuasiveness.

- The paper contains more than five errors in format and written expression, or does not show appropriate changes suggested by the teacher in comments on the first draft.

- The paper uses some of the sources found in the earlier tasks.

(continued)

1 Not meeting the standard(s)

- The changes from the previous draft have not been satisfactorily completed.

- The paper contains many errors in format and written expression or does not relate to the issue described.

- Sources are not properly documented. Most sources found in the earlier tasks are not used.

- The task should be repeated.

Task 8: Create an oral presentation

You are now going to present the information to the policymaker who hired you.

Create a brief (5–10 minutes) presentation including the most important information that would make policymakers want to learn more about this subject—in fact, would make them want to read your paper! You can use visual aids to help illustrate your research and conclusions.

In addition to a classroom presentation, find an appropriate public audience for this issue. Perhaps it is the local school board, city commission, recreation board, League of Women Voters, civic group or other organization. The opportunity to present your research in public is one of the most important ways to show that your research helps to make a real difference.

If it is impossible to find an opportunity to present this information to the public, give the presentation to another class in your school.

Scoring Guide—Task 8

4 Exemplary

- The presentation is clear and persuasive. It is supported by superb graphics. The presenter responds to questions clearly and completely.

- The presentation is ready for consideration by actual policymakers.

(continued)

Research Makes a Difference (continued)

3 Proficient

- The presentation is clear and persuasive, though there are minor errors in expression and visual aids. The presenter responds to most questions clearly and completely.

- The presentation, with minor improvements, is ready for consideration by actual policymakers.

2 Progressing

- The presentation is closely related to the paper, but lacks clarity and persuasiveness. The presenter is unprepared for most questions.

- Substantial revision is necessary before this presentation is ready for consideration by actual policymakers.

1 Not meeting the standard(s)

- The presentation is either poorly related to the paper or the paper on which it is based is unacceptable (please see Task 7).

- The task should be repeated.

(continued)

International Performance Assessment System (IPAS)

Sample Mathematics Assessment

Design the Ideal School

Benchmark Grades: 6-8

Summary:
Students use math skills to draw scale plans for an ideal school.

Keywords:
Geometry
Arithmetic
Measurement
Fractions
Ratios
Communication of results
Drawing
Research skills
Writing skills

Mathematics Standards Addressed:

- Students will draw on a broad body of mathematical knowledge and apply mathematical skills and strategies. This includes using the following: mathematical reasoning, oral and written communication, and the appropriate technology when solving real-world problems.

- Students will use geometric concepts, properties, and relationships in problem-solving situations and communicate the reasoning used in solving these problems.

- Students will use a variety of tools and techniques to measure, apply the results in problem-solving situations, and communicate the reasoning used in solving these problems.

- Students will develop, analyze, and explain procedures for solving problems involving proportions.

(continued)

Design the Ideal School (continued)

Language Arts Standards Addressed:

- Students will read to locate, select, and make use of relevant information from various media, reference, and technological resources.

In addition to standards for mathematics and language arts, students who have completed this project in the past have also demonstrated proficiency in standards related to civics (understanding the role and application of governmental regulation), art (creating a realistic representation of a concept in two and three dimensional models), and communications (presenting an expository oral presentation, which clearly communicates the solution to a complex problem).

Information for the Teacher

- ## TASK DESCRIPTION

  This assessment asks students to apply math skills by planning, designing, and drawing an "ideal" school. Students also research their own school and learn what facilities are needed.

  Students will need access to information about their school, such as the square footage, cost per square foot, number of students/faculty, etc. (see Tasks 3 and 4). You can research this information in advance, or give students ballpark figures/estimations with which to work.

  The amount and level of work for these tasks can be adjusted. For example, you can ask students to research more or less than what is required in the tasks or to calculate the area of irregular geometric shapes. For Task 4, you can ask the students to include more specific data on the square footage of particular parts of the schools.

  For the students who complete Tasks 1 through 5 ahead of the rest of the class, there are enrichment tasks provided at the end of the assessment. Other enrichment possibilities include asking the students to consider the implications of various design choices (one big school vs. two smaller schools) or to trade results with students working in other schools (or even other districts) to assemble a larger set of data.

- ## REQUIRED MATERIALS

  - Graph paper
  - Drawing supplies and tools
  - Access to building professionals (for enrichment tasks)

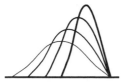

(continued)

Design the Ideal School (continued)

Assessment Introduction—Here is what you will do...

Your job is to design the perfect school. Let your imagination soar. What would the perfect school building look like? Would it have plenty of room for schoolwork and social activities? Would it have room for soccer, baseball, and other sports? Would it be designed so that every student—even those who cannot see, hear, or walk—could easily take advantage of every part of the school?

You are going to design an ideal school. Even though you may like your school as it is, imagine ways it could be better.

This assignment is an opportunity to try out your ideas. The tasks help you organize your ideas. It's important to check with your teacher after you complete each task. Then, when your teacher has evaluated your work, go to the next task.

Task 1: Describe your ideal school

Write a description of your ideal school. Be as specific as you can in your written description. Write exactly what the school will include.

What sorts of things should you include? Think about the activities in your school. Think about the rooms that you need in order to do these activities. Include areas that teachers and the administration of your ideal school would need.

Research by walking around your own school to see what is there.

Once you have your description, draw your ideal school. Your drawing does not have to be a "scale drawing," you will do that in the next task. Show what the school would look like.

Include as much detail as possible in your description and picture. This will help you in later tasks.

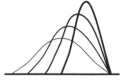

(continued)

Scoring Guide—Task 1

4 Exemplary

- The student writes a description of an ideal school.

- The detailed description contains at least five aspects of the school, including the needs of students and teachers, and describes why these aspects are important.

- Items described include basic needs.

- Spelling and grammatical errors do not significantly affect the communication of ideas.

- The drawing gives a clear picture of the school.

- The response includes more advanced work. For example, the description includes space for "extra" or special needs, needs for school staff, needs for art, music, and other programs. The description is especially thorough, detailed, and clearly communicated.

3 Proficient

- The student writes a description of an ideal school.

- The detailed description contains at least five aspects of the school, including the needs of students and teachers, and describes why these aspects are important.

- Items described include basic needs.

- Spelling and grammatical errors do not significantly affect the communication of ideas.

- The drawing gives a clear picture of the school.

2 Progressing

- The response includes a description of two aspects of an ideal school.

- An explanation is included for the two aspects, but the description does not give enough detail to determine how the student views the school.

- Spelling and grammatical errors make it hard to understand the response.

- The drawing is not detailed enough to give a clear picture of the school.

1 Not meeting the standard(s)

- The description and the drawing are not clear.

- The task should be repeated.

(continued)

Design the Ideal School (continued)

Task 2: Draw a plan of your ideal school

Make a **scale drawing** or plan of your ideal school. To do this, imagine looking down on the school with the roof removed. What would you see?

A scale drawing means that the length of the lines you use on the paper must represent a certain number of feet for the actual building. Use your description and drawing from Task 1 to guide this scale drawing. Show what scale you are using.

Use graph paper to draw your scale model. Label each room. Once you begin drawing, you may realize that you want to include rooms and areas that you did not include in your description and original drawing. You may include those changes now.

Scoring Guide—Task 2

4 Exemplary

- The scale drawing is clear, neat, and directly related to the written description in Task 1.

- The scale is mathematically accurate and consistent.

- A key is provided for the scale, and all rooms and areas are clearly labeled.

- The drawing shows an appropriate level of detail that conveys the ideas in the written description.

- The response includes more advanced work. For example, it includes unique designs, or detailed layouts of certain sections of the school (such as sports facilities or an auditorium)

3 Proficient

- The scale drawing is clear, neat, and directly related to the written description in Task 1.

- The scale is mathematically accurate and consistent.

- A key is provided for the scale, and all rooms and areas are clearly labeled. The drawing shows an appropriate level of detail that conveys the ideas in the written description.

(continued)

Design the Ideal School (continued)

2 Progressing

- The scale drawing shows good ideas, but they are not clearly related to the written description.

- The scale contains some mathematical errors, which make the drawing inaccurate.

- The key is provided but many areas are not clearly labeled.

- More work is needed.

1 Not meeting the standard(s)

- The scale drawing is not consistent with the written description.

- The scale drawing uses an inconsistent scale or the calculations are incorrect.

- The drawing is not labeled and there is no key.

- The task should be repeated.

Task 3: Evaluate your model based on the real thing

It is time to put your model to the test by comparing it to your actual school.

First, make an estimate of how many teachers, staff, and students will use your ideal school building. Show how you arrived at your estimate. Next, consider how you have addressed certain design issues in your ideal school. Answer at least four of the following questions.

- Given the size of your ideal school, how much space is needed for a parking lot, and how many cars will actually be able to park there?

- How wide are the hallways in your ideal school?

- What is the average number of students in each class? How many classrooms will you need?

- How much space is needed for classes that have special equipment such as shop classes, auto classes, chemistry labs, art studios, drama, and band classes?

- How many books and other media should the library have? How much space is needed for that?

(continued)

Design the Ideal School (continued)

- If some of your classmates have physical disabilities and need extra space (for example, to get a wheelchair through a door) or need special help (for example, to have library shelves within reach). Will this change your design?

- How much space is required around the building for the playing fields and other outdoor facilities?

- How many people does the auditorium seat and how big is the stage?

When you have completed your answers you will be given information about your actual school. This might include the number of students, number of rooms, square feet of the building, size of the parking lot, etc. Use this information about your existing school to evaluate your ideal school plan.

Write a brief summary of the differences between your ideal school and your actual school.

Scoring Guide—Task 3

4 Exemplary

- The student uses his/her design to answer the questions in the task.

- The responses relate to the specific design of the school prepared in previous tasks.

- All calculations are correct. Calculations are shown and explained.

- The response contains a clearly written estimate of the people who will use the building.

- The estimate of the number of teachers and staff is consistent with the number of students.

- The summary gives an accurate comparison of the ideal school and the actual school.

- The response includes more advanced work. For example, it includes answers to more than five questions, follow-up questions, or questions that have several related or connected parts.

3 Proficient

- The student uses his/her design to answer the questions in the task.

- The responses relate to the specific design of the school prepared in previous tasks.

- All calculations are correct. Calculations are shown and explained.

(continued)

Design the Ideal School (continued)

- The response contains a clearly written estimate of the people who will use the building.

- The estimate of the number of teachers and staff is consistent with the number of students.

- The summary gives an accurate comparison of the ideal school and the actual school.

2 Progressing

- The student uses his/her design to answer at least one of the questions in the task.

- The responses relate to the specific design of the school prepared in previous tasks.

- Only some of the calculations are correct or calculations are not shown or explained.

- The response contains an estimate of the people who will use the building, but it is not clear how the student arrived at this number and the number is not reasonable (too high or too low given other information).

1 Not meeting the standard(s)

- The response does not meet one or more criteria for a progressing scoring.

- The task should be repeated.

Task 4: How much will your school cost?

Prepare a table comparing your ideal school to your actual school.

The comparison should include the following items:
- Square footage
- Number of students
- Cost per square foot
- Cost per student
- Total cost

You should have data for the actual school. Depending on what questions were answered in Task 3, you may need to make a few more calculations.

(continued)

Design the Ideal School (continued)

You will be given information on the cost of your actual school. Use this data and the information in your table to estimate the cost of your ideal school. Consider how the costs would change due to inflation or to the increased complexity of your new design. Estimate how much your ideal school would cost to build today. Show your calculations.

Scoring Guide—Task 4

4 Exemplary

- The student creates a table containing the data and estimations for his or her ideal school and the data from the real school. All calculations are correct.

- The student compares the estimations with the data.

- The student determines an estimated cost for the ideal school building. The number is reasonable.

- The items in the table are consistent with work in previous tasks or work presented in this task.

- The response includes more advanced work. For example, the student breaks down the cost of the new school and prepares sub-estimates for each part of it, or compares costs of the different parts to the actual school.

3 Proficient

- The student creates a table containing his or her estimations and the data from the real school. All calculations are correct.

- The student compares the estimations with the real data.

- The student determines an estimated cost for the ideal school building. The number is reasonable.

- The items in the table are consistent with work in previous tasks or work presented in this task.

2 Progressing

- The student creates a table containing his or her estimations and the data from the real school. Calculations have minor errors.

- The student compares the estimations with the real data.

(continued)

Design the Ideal School (continued)

- The student determines an estimated cost for the ideal school building. It is not clear how the student determined the estimations and the numbers are not reasonable.

- The items in the table are not consistent with the work in previous tasks.

- More work is needed.

1 Not meeting the standard(s)

- The response does not meet one or more criteria for a proficient scoring.

- The task should be repeated.

Task 5: Improve your plan

Modify and improve your model. Based on your answers in Task 3 and your comparisons, are there changes you would like to make to your model?

Only you can decide how to improve your planned school. This task is for you to step back and look at the big picture. Go back over all the work you have done and ask yourself:

- Are there any holes in my plan? Are there things I forgot to include that would improve the plan?

- Are there any inconsistencies?

- Does something look out of place now?

To improve your plan you might need to do any number of different things: redraw the plan to be clearer, do more research on a question, etc.

Improve your planned school. Update any tables and drawings as necessary.

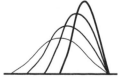

(continued)

Scoring Guide—Task 5

4 Exemplary

- The revised plan is a significant improvement from the first model.

- The plans are rich in detail and based on the research and questions designed by the student.

- All information about the plan is consistent and based on consistent assumptions.

- The scale drawing is clear and neat.

- The scale is mathematically accurate and consistent.

- The scale is shown.

- The plan includes changes that include all of the work done in Task 4.

- All calculations are accurate and documented.

- The response includes more advanced work. For example, the student conducts additional research to improve or redesign a key aspect of the plan and includes all of the things described in Task 1.

3 Proficient

- The revised plan is a clear and significant improvement from the first model.

- The plans are rich in detail and based on the research and questions designed by the student.

- All information about the plan is consistent and based on consistent assumptions.

- The scale drawing is clear and neat.

- The scale is mathematically accurate and consistent.

- The scale is shown.

- The plan includes changes that include all of the work done in Task 4.

- All calculations are accurate and documented.

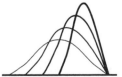

(continued)

Design the Ideal School (continued)

2 Progressing

- The revised plan is an improvement, but contains errors in mathematical scale and lacks a clear connection to the research conducted by the student.

- More work is needed.

1 Not meeting the standard(s)

- The revised plan is not an improvement over the first draft.

- The task should be repeated.

Enrichment Task 1: A three-dimensional model

Based on your improved drawing in Task 5, create a three-dimensional model of your ideal school. Using materials approved by your teacher, create a sturdy, portable model.

You may decide that there are some more changes you want to make in your model. You can do that, but document all of your changes and make sure your model on paper agrees with your three-dimensional model.

Present your model to the class with explanations of your design.

Scoring Guide—Enrichment Task 1

4 Exemplary

- The model is accurate in all dimensions.

- The oral presentation is well researched, organized, and clear.

- The response includes more advanced work. For example, the student prepares computer generated three-dimensional color drawings or drawings with overlays.

3 Proficient

- The model is accurate in all dimensions.

- The oral presentation is well researched, organized, and clear.

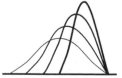

(continued)

Design the Ideal School (continued)

2 Progressing

- The model is accurate in two dimensions, but the third dimension departs significantly from the written plan.

- The oral presentation is not clearly based on student research and is unclear.

1 Not meeting the standard(s)

- The model is not an accurate representation of the student's design.

- The presentation is not clearly linked to the model.

Enrichment Task 2: Get expert feedback

Share your model with an architect or engineer. Ask this professional to look at your design and make recommendations for further improvement.

Be sure to do the following:

- Give the professional all of the work you did, including all the tasks of the project, from the initial planning through the improvements and changes you made.

- Show the professional how you conducted research to support your final design.

- Send a thank-you note after the interview.

Based on the feedback you receive from the professional, write your reflections on what you would do differently if you were to approach this project again.

Your teacher will explain how to contact the professional architect or engineer.

Scoring Guide—Enrichment Task 2

4 Exemplary

- The student presents his or her work to an expert.

- The student summarizes the feedback and decides what would be different next time.

- The response includes more advanced work. For example, the student discusses several options for improvements and why some might be better than others.

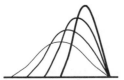

(continued)

3 Proficient

- The student presents his or her work to an expert.

- The student summarizes the feedback and decides what would be different next time.

2 Progressing

- The student presents his or her work to an expert.

- The student summarizes the feedback, but does not include specifics offered in the feedback.

- More work is needed.

1 Not meeting the standard(s)

- The student's reflection does not include the comments from the professional.

- More work is needed.

International Performance Assessment System (IPAS)

Sample Social Studies Assessment

Design and Build Your Own Town

Benchmark Grades: Upper Elementary

Summary:
Students design their own settlement using blocks and compare it to Jamestown or other early settlements.

Keywords:
Early American history
Working in groups
Problem solving
Measurement
Spatial organization

Social Studies Standards Addressed:

- Student will show the process, patterns, and functions of human settlement.

- Students will know how to analyze the spatial organization of people, places, and environments.

- Students will demonstrate an understanding of how ideas, conditions, and people change over time to develop historical perspective.

- Students will understand historical development and know the characteristics of various economic systems.

- Students will demonstrate an understanding that differing values and opposing goals can result in conflict, which requires tolerance and cooperation for resolution.

Mathematics Standards Addressed:

- The student will apply measurement concepts in solving problems.

- Students will use geometric concepts, properties, and relationships in problem-solving situations and communicate the reasoning used in solving these problems.

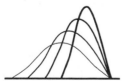

(continued)

Information for the Teacher

- **TASK DESCRIPTION**

  Students will work within groups to design a town using building blocks. They are asked to apply what they have learned about early American settlements in designing their own settlement.

  An enrichment task is included after the four assessment tasks.

- **REQUIRED MATERIALS**

  Each group will need a base for the settlement with physical characteristics, such as rivers, mountains, and an ocean. Provide four different colors of blocks. Students will also need a detailed map of the Jamestown settlement or of another early settlement your class has been studying.

Assessment Introduction—Here is what you will do...

Your class is studying about European settlers arriving in America. You are probably studying early settlements, such as Jamestown. What might that have been like? Since towns as we know them were not already built when they arrived, how did the settlers decide where to live and work? How did they know where to put their roads, houses, farms, churches, schools, and other buildings? How did the landscape affect their choices? How did their choices affect the lives of Native American people who were already in the area?

Here is your chance to travel back in time. For this assignment, imagine being alive during the time when places like Jamestown were being settled. You and your group will re-create the settlers' experience by using colored blocks to build a town. Your teacher will provide you with a base for your town. This base will tell you about the landscape and show you the location of rivers, mountains, and an ocean.

Task 1: Design a town

You have a base that tells you where rivers, mountains, and an ocean are located. If you were a settler here, where would you want the center of town to be? Where would you plan to plant your crops? Are there already people living in the area?

- As a group, decide where the town will be located. Brainstorm all the things a town needs, such as a school, church, farms, roads, houses, gardens to grow food, etc. Consider how the landscape will affect your town plan. Decide where **each part** of the town will be located.

(continued)

Design and Build Your Own Town (continued)

- Draw a plan of your town. Each person in your group should have a drawing, but they should all be similar.

- Using blocks as buildings, make a model of your town.

- On your own piece of paper, write down the parts of the town that you included. Write down where you located each part of town and why your group chose this location. Include as much detail as possible.

Scoring Guide—Task 1

4 Exemplary

- The student works with a group to decide the layout of the town.

- The student draws and builds the plan based on the discussion in the group. The drawing and the block models are clear and understandable.

- The town plan is based in part on what the student has learned about life in an early settlement. It is detailed.

- A written description is included. The reasons for the location of each part of the town are given. The decisions make sense based on life in the early settlement.

- More advanced work is include. For example, the student draws on previous knowledge of this period in history and uses detailed and accurate examples in his or her description of why locations were chosen. The student addressed how the settlers' country of origin might have affected their choices.

3 Proficient

- The student works with a group to decide the layout of the town.

- The student draws the plan based on the discussion in the group. The drawing is clear and understandable.

- The town plan is based in part on what the student has learned about life in an early settlement. It is detailed.

- A written description is included. The reasons for the location of each part of the town are given. The decisions make sense based on life in the early settlement.

(continued)

Design and Build Your Own Town (continued)

2 Progressing

- The student works with a group to decide the layout of the town.

- The student draws the plan based on the discussion in the group. The drawing is missing parts or is unclear.

- A written description is included. The description is unclear or incomplete. Not all of the reasons for the location of each part of the town are given.

- Decisions are given that do not make sense based on life in the early settlement.

- The drawing and written description need to be revised.

1 Not meeting the standard(s)

- The assignment is only partially completed, or the drawing and written response are so unclear they cannot be understood.

- The task should be repeated.

Task 2: Is this a good change?

There are many ways that a town can be designed. You can see that every town differs in some ways but is the same in other ways. Even in your group there were probably disagreements about where to locate different parts of the town. Here is your chance to evaluate your settlement.

Your teacher will suggest a change to the plan you have drawn and built. You won't really have to change your town, but think about what would happen if you did. Is the change a good idea or a bad idea? Discuss the following questions with your group.

1) Would the change improve the town plan or not?

2) What other things in the town would change?

3) By making the change, how would it affect the people who live inside **and** outside of the settlement?

When you are finished discussing these questions with your group, go back to your seat and write a report about what your group thinks. In your report, explain what the teacher's change was and how your group addressed the suggested change. Write your opinion if it differs from the group decision. You can also draw a map to describe the change.

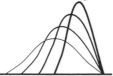

(continued)

Scoring Guide—Task 2

4 Exemplary

- The student takes part in a group discussion about the change.

- The student describes the change and decides if the change would be good or bad for the settlement. The decision is reasonable.

- The report describes at least three other things that would also change. The report describes how life would be different inside and outside the settlement because of this change.

- The student considers the historical time in his or her report.

- The report is clearly written and understandable.

- There are no errors in spelling and punctuation.

- The report includes advanced work. For example, the student considers ways to make the change in the plan work. The student gives at least two alternatives to the change that would improve the settlement.

3 Proficient

- The student takes part in a group discussion about the change.

- The student describes the change and decides if the change would be good or bad for the settlement. The decision is reasonable.

- The report describes at least three other things that would also change. The report describes how life would be different inside and outside the settlement because of this change.

- The student considers the historical time in his or her report.

- The report is clearly written and understandable.

- There are no errors in spelling and punctuation.

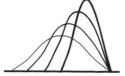

(continued)

2 Progressing

- The student takes part in a group discussion about the change.

- The student decides if the change would be good or bad for the settlement.

- The report includes one thing that would also change.

- The report describes how life would be different inside the settlement, but does not include what might change outside of the settlement. There are parts of the report that are unclear.

- There are errors in spelling and punctuation.

- Some revising is needed.

1 Not meeting the standard(s)

- The student takes part in a group discussion about the change.

- No opinion is given about the change in the report.

- The report contains errors and cannot be understood. The task should be repeated.

Task 3: Design the buildings for your town

There is a reason why a building or an area is a certain size. What would happen if a farm were very small? Would a farmer have enough land to grow crops? What if it were too big? How would that affect other people in the area?

Just as before, when you designed your town, now your group will determine each building's size and shape. For this task, the word "buildings" will be used for all of the parts of your town, including farms.

- Decide how the building will be used. This will determine its shape. For example, should the building be a square or a rectangle?

- Decide how big it should be compared to the other buildings. For example, should the farm be twice as big as a school or only half as big?

- Draw all of the buildings in your town. Label the length and the width of each. Try to draw them "to scale." That means if you multiplied the length and the width of the buildings in your drawing by the number on your scale, you would find the actual size of the buildings in your town.

(continued)

- Each person in your group should have separate drawings, but the buildings should be similar in size and shape.

- Back at your seat, write down the choices your group made. If you disagree with a decision, write down what you think.

Scoring Guide—Task 3

4 Exemplary

- The student takes part in a group that decides the shape and size of all buildings in the settlement. The sizes and shapes of the buildings are all reasonable based on the use of the building.

- The student draws the buildings. The drawing is clear and buildings are labeled.

- A written description of the decisions is given. The description is clear and understandable.

- There are no errors in spelling or grammar.

- More advanced work is included. For example, the student draws the buildings to scale and includes the landscape where the buildings will be located. The student compares and contrasts the opinions of group members. The student considers the effects of the size and shape of each area on people living both inside and outside the settlement. The description is exceptionally clear.

3 Proficient

- The student takes part in a group that decides the shape and size of all buildings in the settlement. The sizes and shapes of the buildings are all reasonable based on the use of the building.

- The student draws the buildings. The drawing is clear and buildings are labeled.

- A written description of the decisions is given. The description is clear and understandable.

- There are no errors in spelling or grammar.

(continued)

2 Progressing

- The student takes part in a group that decides the shape and size of all buildings in the settlement. Some of the sizes and shapes of the buildings are all reasonable based on the use of the building.

- The student draws the buildings. The drawing is unclear or not labeled.

- A written description of the decisions is given but is not clear.

- There are errors in spelling or grammar.

1 Not meeting the standard(s)

- Student takes part in a group that decides the shape and size of all buildings in the settlement. However, the drawing and description are so unclear that they cannot be read. They should be redone.

Task 4: Compare your town

As you are finding out, there is a lot involved in designing and building a town! What have you learned? Sometimes it is important to check your work and ideas with what others have done. This is a good way to share your great ideas and also to learn about things you had not thought of before. In this task you will have the chance to compare your town to other models in your class and to a real settlement.

Trade towns! Go around the classroom and examine the other towns that were designed. Look for ways that groups designed their towns differently. Look for ways they are the same. Discuss these similarities and differences with your group. Go back to your seat and write about the different towns. Should you add to or change your town? Why or why not?

Now compare the town that your group designed to a map of an early settlement such as Jamestown. You may also read a description of the area. Write about the choices that you made. Are they the same as or different than the choices made by the settlers?

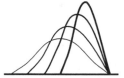

(continued)

Scoring Guide—Task 4

4 Exemplary

- Towns are examined for similarities and differences. The student writes about at least five similarities and differences.

- The student decides if changes should be made to the settlement based on these comparisons. The descriptions are accurate and clearly written.

- Maps are used to compare the settlement with a real town. The settlement is compared and contrasted to the model.

- There are no errors in spelling or grammar.

- Advanced work is included. For example, the student draws on previous knowledge of this period in history and uses examples in his or her description of why locations were chosen in the different settlements.

3 Proficient

- Towns are examined for similarities and differences. The student writes about at least five similarities and differences.

- The student decides if changes should be made to the settlement based on these comparisons. The descriptions are accurate and clearly written.

- Maps are used to compare the settlement with a real town. The settlement is compared and contrasted to the model.

- There are no errors in spelling or grammar.

2 Progressing

- The student compares the towns, but fewer than two similarities and differences are described. The description is unclear.

- Maps are used to compare the settlement with a real town. The settlement is compared and contrasted to the model, but the differences are not evaluated.

- More work is required.

(continued)

Design and Build Your Own Town (continued)

1 Not meeting the standard(s)

- The towns are not compared for similarities or differences. Or the differences are not evaluated.

- Maps are not used to examine the real settlement.

- The task should be repeated.

Task 5: Allocate resources (Enrichment task)

As your town is being built, you and the other settlers (your group members) may disagree about who will use different areas of land or what building materials will be used. How will the town handle problems like this?

- Develop a plan for deciding how the resources will be used if there is a disagreement. Explain why you think the plan will work.

- Write this method down and use it if any disagreements come up among the settlers.

Scoring Guide—Task 5

4 Exemplary

- A plan is developed that will be used to solve disagreements among settlers. The plan is reasonable and fair. The reasons why this plan was chosen are explained in detail.

- There are no errors in spelling or grammar.

- Other possible methods are also discussed with the reasons why those methods were not selected. The student gives an exceptional description of the plan and draws on previous knowledge about the sharing of available resources.

3 Proficient

- A plan is developed that will be used to solve disagreements among settlers. The plan is reasonable and fair. The reasons why this plan was chosen are explained in detail.

- There are no errors in spelling or grammar.

(continued)

Design and Build Your Own Town (continued)

2 Progressing

- A plan is developed that will be used to solve disagreements among settlers. The plan is not fair to all settlers, or is unclear and cannot be followed. The reasons why this plan was chosen are not explained clearly.

- There are errors in spelling or grammar.

- The plan needs revising.

1 Not meeting the standard(s)

- A plan is not developed, does not make sense, or cannot be read.

(continued)

International Performance Assessment System

Sample Science Assessment

The Visitor's Guide to the Solar System

Benchmark Grades: Can be adapted to all elementary grades.

Summary:
Students will look at the solar system as if they are writing a travel guide for alien visitors. They will present facts about our solar system and the movement of the Earth in the solar system. Space exploration will also be addressed.

Keywords:
Solar system
Space exploration
Earth's rotation and revolution
Seasons
Writing skills

Science Standards Addressed:

- Students will explore, demonstrate, communicate, apply and evaluate knowledge of the structure and systems of the Earth and other bodies in the universe.

- Students will understand and explain how components of the Earth and space systems change over time.

- Students will identify characteristics of Earth and space systems that are observable and measurable.

Language Arts Standards Addressed:

- Students will write clearly and effectively to share information and knowledge, influence, create, and entertain for a variety of audiences and purposes.

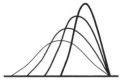

(continued)

Information for the Teacher

- ### TASK DESCRIPTION

The observation of the night sky has fascinated humans for as long as history has been recorded. Before scientific instruments, the sky and its changes were observed with the naked eye. We often ignore what can be seen in the sky, but a mature awareness of the world includes knowledge of the larger universe in which we move.

This assessment focuses on students' awareness of their place in the solar system. The "visitor's guide" metaphor should help students to collect and integrate their work, but it should not be allowed to dominate the content of the assessment.

For Task 3, you can suggest which space exploration events should be covered based on what is happening at the time the assessment is done, or what has been studied in class.

- ### REQUIRED MATERIALS

Reference materials on the solar system, Earth's movement, space exploration, and the Earth's atmosphere are needed.

- ### SCORING KEY FOR THE TEACHER

Answers will vary.

Assessment Introduction—Here is what you will do...

An intergalactic committee of travel agents has decided that their guidebook to the solar system is hopelessly out of date. Therefore, they have hired you to write a new one.

Don't worry about the cover and the index. Focus on the contents of the book. Using your own knowledge and appropriate reference material, you will prepare a guide that will help aliens who visit our solar system find their way around.

These alien visitors have certain needs. Each of the tasks describes one of them.

Task 1: The big picture

Our visiting friends have to navigate into the solar system and find Earth without bumping into things.

(continued)

The Visitor's Guide to the Solar System (continued)

Write the first section of your guidebook. Tell the aliens about any significant objects or bodies in the solar system, their relationship to each other, and their locations. What else can you include in this section? What is it like out there?

Write a title for this section of the guidebook. Illustrate it with at least one picture.

Scoring Guide—Task 1

4 Exemplary

- The student prepares a section of the book that describes all of the major elements of the solar system (the sun, planets and their moons). The description is complete and correct.

- The student tells how these elements are related and where they are located.

- A title and an illustration for the section of the guidebook are included.

- More advanced work is included. For example, "minor" elements such as comets or meteors are described. The section of the book describes the three-dimensional nature of the solar system.

3 Proficient

- The student prepares a section of the book that describes all of the major elements of the solar system (the sun, planets and their moons). The description is complete and correct.

- The student tells how these elements are related and where they are located.

- A title and an illustration for the section of the guidebook are included.

2 Progressing

- The student prepares a section of the book that describes at least three of the major elements of the solar system (the sun, planets and their moons). The description is correct but more detail is needed.

- The description of how these elements are related and where they are located is not complete.

- A title and an illustration for the section of the guidebook are included.

- More work is needed.

(continued)

The Visitor's Guide to the Solar System (continued)

1 Not meeting the standard(s)

- The student prepares a section of the book that describes one element of the solar system. The description is missing important information and detail. Some of the information is incorrect.

- The description of how these elements are related and where they are located is missing.

- A title and/or an illustration for the section of the guidebook are missing.

- The task should be repeated.

Task 2: Taking a closer look

Earth is a big tourist attraction in the solar system, so spend more time describing how to find Earth. (Apparently, it moves—what does it move around?)

In the next section of your guidebook, explain how this movement of Earth produces day and night, the seasons, and the length of the year.

Our visitors think that having the temperature change all the time is rather strange, so be sure to explain to them why that happens.

Give this section a title and illustrate it with a picture.

Scoring Guide—Task 2

4 Exemplary

- The student explains the movements of Earth and how the aliens could locate it.

- The student explains how day and night, the seasons, and the length of the year are related to the Earth and the sun.

- The student explains changes in temperature over time.

- All of the information is correct.

- A title and illustration are included.

- The section includes advanced work. For example, the descriptions are especially detailed, creative, and accurate.

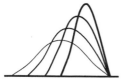

(continued)

The Visitor's Guide to the Solar System (continued)

3 Proficient

- The student explains the movements of Earth and how the aliens could locate it.

- The student explains how day and night, the seasons, and the length of the year are related to the Earth and the sun.

- The student explains changes in temperature over time.

- All of the information is correct.

- A title and illustration are included.

2 Progressing

- The student partially explains the movements of Earth and how the aliens could locate it.

- The student partially explains how day and night, the seasons, and the length of the year are related to the Earth and the sun.

- The student partially explains changes in temperature over time.

- The information contains errors and lacks detail, or the descriptions are incomplete.

- A title and illustration are included.

- More work is needed.

1 Not meeting the standard(s)

- The descriptions are incomplete or contain a significant amount of error.

- The title and illustration are missing.

- The task should be repeated.

Task 3: Space (traffic) jam

You wouldn't want our alien friends hitting anything made by humans on their trip through the solar system, so you should advise them about any "traffic" among the planets that humans have created.

Are there any space exploration projects going on now?

Are there any satellites in space that they need to avoid?

(continued)

The Visitor's Guide to the Solar System (continued)

Visitors find our efforts in space travel rather cute, so if we have just completed a space exploration project, you should tell them about that as well.

What will you name this section of your book? Don't forget your illustration.

Scoring Guide—Task 3

4 Exemplary

- The student describes any recent or upcoming space exploration event. The description is detailed and includes such things as its purpose, timing, and path through the solar system.

- The description includes other human made objects in space such as satellites.

- More advanced work is included. For example, the student gives the aliens a history of space exploration in this section and describes what the aliens would have seen during various times in history. The student includes space exploration from other countries.

3 Proficient

- The student describes any recent or upcoming space exploration event. The description is detailed and includes such things as its purpose, timing, and path through the solar system.

- The description includes other human made objects in space such as satellites.

2 Progressing

- The student describes at least one space exploration event. The description lacks detail (includes general comments such as "we went to the moon," or "watch out for the space shuttle"). Other human made objects are not included in the description.

- More work is needed.

1 Not meeting the standard(s)

- The student does not use a real-life space exploration event in the section, but includes a made-up event. The task was not completed.

- The task should be repeated.

(continued)

The Visitor's Guide to the Solar System (continued)

Task 4: Culture shock

Our visitors have never been on a planet with this type of atmosphere.

They don't understand this day/night thing and why it changes what you can see in the sky.

Try to explain what you can see from Earth looking at the sky both during the day and at night. Describe what you see that moves. Explain why these things move.

Include a title and illustration.

Scoring Guide—Task 4

4 Exemplary

- The section describes the contents of the daytime sky (sun, moon, some planets) and the nighttime sky (moon, planets, stars, constellations). The description is accurate and complete.

- The student gives an accurate explanation of the movement of celestial bodies as seen from Earth.

- A title and illustration are included.

- The section includes advanced work. For example, the Earth/sun description includes ideas such as the different timing of seasons in the north and south, and the sky descriptions include seasonal or occasional events. The student explains the differences between atmospheric events from celestial ones.

3 Proficient

- The section describes the contents of the daytime sky (sun, moon, some planets) and the nighttime sky (moon, planets, stars, constellations). The description is accurate and complete.

- The student gives an accurate explanation of the movement of celestial bodies as seen from Earth.

- A title and illustration are included.

(continued)

The Visitor's Guide to the Solar System (continued)

2 Progressing

- The section describes at least one element of the daytime and nighttime skies. Some of the information is incorrect, or the description is missing obvious or important elements.

- Some understanding is shown of the connection between the movements of the Earth and changes in what can be seen in the sky.

- More work is needed.

1 Not meeting the standard(s)

- The section is incomplete or one element of the daytime or the nighttime sky is included, but not all. There is not enough detail.

- The connection between movements of the Earth and changes in what can be seen in the sky is not explained.

- There is no title or illustration.

- The task should be repeated.

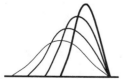

(continued)

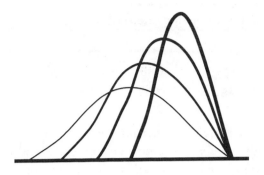

Appendix B

Staff Development Curriculum

School districts may select from the following workshops to customize a year-long staff development curriculum. These staff development offerings include the core curriculum—knowledge that every teacher and administrator should have to obtain a fundamental mastery of standards-based performance assessments. In addition, these offerings include an enrichment curriculum—workshops that are available on specific topics to assist teachers in the development and implementation of standards-based performance assessments for use in their classroom. Each workshop is scheduled for two hours. The workshops can also be extended and combined to allow additional hands-on participation. We can schedule workshops ranging in length from day long sessions to weeklong institutes. We can customize a Staff Development Plan to meet your needs. This is the kind of comprehensive staff development that the Center for Performance Assessment has implemented in school districts all across the country. More than just theory, our staff development focus provides practical, hands-on experience that moves the standards initiative in your district forward.

Core Curriculum

▓ MSW 101: Why Standards?

Why Standards? Because they are fair and because they work! This course will present evidence in support of these ideas as well as introduce the legislative and educational rationale for standards. In addition, the fundamental differences between the standards-based approach to education and the traditional approaches as well as the differences between standards and norms will be discussed. The crucial issue of expectations—by teachers, by students, by parents and the community— is a vital component of standards-based education.

■ MSW 102: Goals for Classroom Assessment

This course identifies the criteria teachers will use to screen assignments and assessments used in their classrooms. It is designed to make the teacher a "critical consumer" of both outside materials and teacher created materials used for assignments and assessments. Practical suggestions will be presented to assist teachers in designing assignments and assessments that are challenging and engaging to students.

■ MSW 103: Introduction to Performance Assessment

This course introduces the form and construction of performance assessments. Are all "alternative assessments" performance assessments? This question as well as others will be answered. This course is designed to assist teachers with the integration of assessment and instructional practice in the classroom. The differences between traditional and performance assessment will be discussed. Practical applications for the classroom will be modeled including the identification of standards, activities and the evaluation criteria to be used to develop performance assessments.

■ MSW 104: Developing Scoring Guides

This course focuses on the development of meaningful, specific, and mutually exclusive scoring guides (rubrics) for performance assessment. The question, "Why use scoring guides?" will be answered. Sample scoring guides will be critiqued and suggestions will be offered to assist teachers in the creation of scoring guides. The extended version offers participants the opportunity to create a scoring guide to be used in their classroom.

■ MSW 105: Portfolio Assessment

This course focuses on the design, assembly, and scoring of portfolios. A distinction is made between a student's "working file" and a portfolio that is used to demonstrate proficiency in relation to standards. Practical ideas will be offered to increase the effectiveness of the portfolio as an assessment instrument.

■ MSW 106: Grading and Standards—Working Together

This course addresses the issues involved with incorporating standards-based performance and traditional grades. What kinds of changes need to be made in a traditional grading system to reflect a student's level of proficiency, not just their "letter" grade? A Standards Achievement Report will be discussed.

■ MSW 107: Equity Issues in Assessment

This course focuses on the imperative of equity in assessment design and the creation of "opportunities to learn" for all students. This course will include principle of equity, as well as the importance of variable time, fixed learning for students. Suggestions will be offered to assist teachers in maintaining equity in their classrooms and in their teaching. Examples of assessment strategies, and accommodations in assessment will be discussed.

■ MSW 108: Designing Performance Assessments

This course considers the practical issues of the construction and evaluation of performance assessments. Ten steps to creating effective performance assessments will be presented and modeled. The participants will begin the construction of their own performance assessment.

■ MSW 109: Technology, Assessment and Standards

This course focuses on ways of using technology in the assessment process and for implementing standards. How can teachers use existing technology to help improve instruction, to make lessons more engaging for students, and to facilitate the integration of assessment into the instructional process? Specific ideas will be presented to help decrease the level of anxiety often associated with discussions of technology.

■ MSW 110: Designing a Standards-Based Classroom

This course will describe how a standards-based classroom differs from a traditional classroom. Specific strategies will be presented to help teachers make standards-based education a reality in their classroom. Suggestions for involving students in standards implementation will be discussed. The classroom becomes an environment in which learning is the focus for everyone, not simply the teacher teaching and the students learning.

■ MSW 111: Beyond Bloom—Learning Performance at High Levels of Application

This course will describe the importance of real world applications in teaching and learning. Students are more likely to stay engaged in the learning process when we increase the relevancy of instructional tasks. This becomes imperative if we are to raise expectations for our students and provide opportunities for success. Suggestions will be presented to help teachers expand current curriculum, rather effortlessly, to reflect real world applications.

■ MSW 112: Designing Standards-Based Performance Assessments

This course presents a specific plan for designing standards-based performance assessments. Each step is clearly explained and then modeled for the participants. Participants are then encouraged to design their own performance assessments within the supportive environment offered in the workshop setting.

■ MSW 113: Teaching Strategies for Implementing Standards

This workshop will present the idea that teachers will need to expand their repertoire of teaching strategies if the implementation of standards will become a reality. Practical ideas will assist teachers in designing lesson plans that focus on student achievement and real world applications. How can we redesign our current instructional ideas to raise expectations for our students and provide them with the tools they will need to meet our expectations for them?

■ MSW 114: Aligning Curriculum and Instruction to Standards

This workshop presents a model for aligning existing curriculum with standards. Hallmarks of effective standards-based instruction will be discussed as well as instructional planning that will provide students with the "Opportunity to Learn". Practical ideas that address the seamless integration between curriculum, instruction and assessment will be discussed. The next step is to design or craft instruction that is aligned with both the curriculum and standards. The role of resources, both traditional and electronic, will be discussed.

Enrichment Curriculum

Assignments and Assessments—These workshops focus on specific subject areas and specific grade levels to assist teachers in creating standards-based performance assessments and classroom assignments in specialized areas for immediate use by the participants.

MSW 201	Elementary Math
MSW 202	Elementary Language Arts
MSW 203	Elementary Science
MSW 204	Elementary Social Studies
MSW 205	Elementary Multi-Disciplinary
MSW 206	Middle School Math
MSW 207	Middle School Language Arts
MSW 208	Middle School Science
MSW 209	Middle School Social Studies
MSW 210	Middle School Multi-Disciplinary
MSW 211	High School Math
MSW 212	High School Language Arts
MSW 213	High School Science
MSW 214	High School Social Studies
MSW 215	High School Multi-Disciplinary

■ For additional information, please call:

Donna M. Davis, M.Ed.
Director, Professional Development
(800) THINK-99 ■ (303) 504-9312

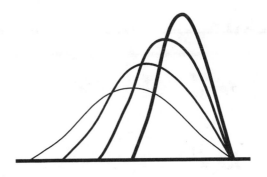

Appendix C

Standards Implementation Checklist

Classroom Checklist

Professional Practice	Exemplary	Proficient	Progressing	Remarks
1. Standards are highly visible in the classroom. The standards are expressed in language that the students understand.				
2. Examples of "exemplary" student work are displayed throughout the classroom.				
3. Students can spontaneously explain what "proficient" work means for each assignment.				
4. For every assignment, project, or test, the teacher publishes in advance the explicit expectations for "proficient" work.				
5. Student evaluation is always done according to the standards and scoring guide criteria and *never* done based on a "curve."				
6. The teacher can explain to any parent or other stakeholder the specific expectations of students for the year.				
7. The teacher has the flexibility to vary the length and quantity of curriculum content on a day to day basis in order to insure that students receive more time on the most critical subjects.				
8. Commonly used standards, such as those for written expression, are reinforced in every subject area. In other words, "spelling always counts"—even in math, science, music and every other discipline.				
9. The teacher has created at least one standards-based performance assessment in the past month.				

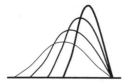

(continued)

Professional Practice	Exemplary	Proficient	Progressing	Remarks
10. The teacher exchanges student work (accompanied by a scoring guide) with a colleague for review and evaluation at least once every two weeks.				
11. The teacher provides feedback to students and parents about the quality of student work compared to the standards—not compared to other students.				
12. The teacher helps to build a community consensus in the classroom and with other stakeholders for standards and high expectations of all students.				
13. The teacher uses a variety of assessment techniques, including (but not limited to) extended written responses, in all disciplines.				
14. Other professional practices appropriate for your classroom:				

School Checklist

Professional Practice	Exemplary	Proficiency	Progressing	Remarks
1. A Standards/Class matrix (standards across the top, classes on the left side) is in a prominent location. Each box indicates the correspondence between a class and the standards. Faculty members and school leaders discuss areas of overlap and standards that are not sufficiently addressed.				
2. Standards are visible throughout the school and in every classroom.				
3. The school leaders use every opportunity for parent communication to build a community consensus for rigorous standards and high expectations for all students.				
4. Information about rigorous standards and high expectations is a specific part of the agenda of every faculty meeting, site council meeting, and parent organization meeting.				
5. The principal personally evaluates some student projects or papers compared to a school-wide or district-wide standard.				
6. The principal personally evaluates selected student portfolios compared to a school-wide or district-wide standard.				
7. Examples of "exemplary" student papers are highly visible.				
8. Job interview committees explicitly inquire about the views of a candidate about standards, performance assessment, and instructional methods for helping all students achieve high standards.				

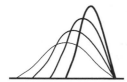

(continued)

Professional Practice	Exemplary	Proficiency	Progressing	Remarks
9. A "jump-start" program is available to enhance the professional education of new teachers who do not have an extensive background in standards and assessment techniques.				
10. Every discretionary dollar spent on staff development and instructional support is specifically linked to student achievement, high standards, and improved assessment.				
11. Faculty meetings are used for structured collaboration with a focus on student work—not for the making of announcements.				
12. The principal personally reviews the assessment and instructional techniques used by teachers as part of the personnel review and evaluation process. The principal specifically considers the link between teacher assessments and standards.				
13. Other professional practices appropriate for your school:				

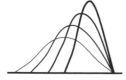

District/State/System Checklist

Professional Practice	Exemplary	Proficient	Progressing	Remarks
1. The system has an accountability plan that is linked to student achievement of standards—not to the competition of schools with one another.				
2. The system has a program for monitoring the "antecedents of excellence"—that is, the strategies that schools use to achieve high standards. The monitoring system does not depend on test scores alone.				
3. The system explicitly authorizes teachers to modify the curriculum guides in quantity and emphasis so that student needs for core academic requirements in math, science, language arts and social studies are met.				
4. The system publishes the "best practices in standards-based assessment" on an annual basis, recognizing the creative efforts of teachers and administrators.				
5. The system has established an assessment task force to monitor the implementation of effective and fair assessments, and to distribute models of educational assessments for use throughout the year.				
6. The system provides timely feedback on district-level assessments so that all assessments can be used to inform instruction during the current school year. Assessments that are not used for the purpose of informing instruction and improving student achievement are not used.				

(continued)

Professional Practice	Exemplary	Proficient	Progressing	Remarks
7. The system reports to the public a comprehensive set of student achievement results throughout the year.				
8. The system uses multiple methods of assessments for system-wide assessments. It never relies on a single indicator or single assessment method to represent student achievement.				
9. There is a clearly identified senior leader at the system level who is responsible for standards, assessment, and accountability, and who communicates this information clearly to all stakeholders.				
10. Commitment to standards is a criteria in all hiring decisions at all levels.				
11. The system monitors the investment of resources—including staff development, technology, and capital expenditures—for a consistent and clear link to student achievement of standards. System leaders can provide explicit examples of changes in resource allocation decisions that reflect this commitment.				
12. Evaluations of schools and of building leaders are based on student achievement—not based on competition or any other norm-referenced system.				

(continued)

Professional Practice	Exemplary	Proficient	Progressing	Remarks
13. The system does not take into account ethnicity and socio-economic level in determining its expectations of student performance. These variables, along with linguistic background, learning disabilities, and other factors, are included in resource allocation decisions and the development of instructional and assessment strategies.				
14. The system allocates resources based on student needs and a commitment to the opportunity for all students to achieve standards. Resources are not allocated merely on the basis of student population—the objective is equity of opportunity, not equality of distribution.				
15. Other professional practices appropriate for your system:				

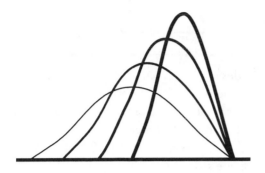

Glossary

Academic (or Content) Standards

The knowledge and skills expected of students at certain stages in their education. In other words, academic content standards describe what students should know and be able to do.

Accountability

The obligation of reporting, explaining, or justifying standards, making them responsible, explicable and answerable.

Assessment

An appraisal or evaluation.

Assignment

A particular task or job given to a student for a specific purpose.

Central Tendency

The score of a typical individual in a group. The mean (or average), median, and mode are measures commonly used to report the central tendency of test scores.

Concurrent Validity Tests

Comparison of district-wide tests (involving a sample of students) with the Standards Achievement Report for those students. If the teacher-designed assessments are based on the same standards of performance as the district assessments, the results should be consistent in a high percentage of cases. Any disparities should be investigated.

Evaluation

An appraisal (examination or test) to determine progress of a student toward meeting academic standards.

Inter-Rater Reliability

A term used to describe the relationship of the scores (ratings) among two or more judges (raters). This can be computed in a variety of ways from simple correlations to percentage of agreement. The larger numbers indicate a greater degree of agreement.

Modeling

Teaching methods and resources that serve as an example for imitation and comparison.

Network

A widespread, organized system of people who can serve as a resource for standards implementation.

Norm

A designated standard average performance.

Performance Assessment

An evaluation (or examination) used to determine a student's progress toward meeting academic standards.

Performance Standards

The levels of performance of tasks that students must reach to demonstrate they have met the Content Standards—or that they are on their way toward meeting them. Performance Standards can be distinguished from Content Standards because Performance Standards have levels (e.g., 4 = exemplary, 3 = proficient, 2 = progressing, 1 = not meeting the standards).

Reliability

In order for a measure to be reliable it must be consistent.

Reliability Coefficient

A measure of how two judges score the same exam. A reliability coefficient of 1.0 means they are in complete 100% agreement.

Psychometrician

A person who designs mathematical and statistical tests to measure psychological variables such as intelligence, aptitude, and emotional disturbance.

Pilot Project

An experimental or trial undertaking of standards implementation prior to full-scale use.

Rubric

The specific rules within the scoring guide. For example, one Language Arts rubric might be to "read and recognize literature as an expression of human experience." These also appear on the Standards Achievement Report.

Scenario

An outline or dramatic plot or situation.

Scoring Guides

The documents used to determine whether the work is exemplary, proficient, progressing toward the standard, or not yet meeting the standard. A Standards Achievement Report (SAR) is an example of one such guide.

Standard

A model that is used as a basis of judgment.

Standards Achievement Report (SAR)

One type of scoring guide designed to replace the traditional report card, consisting of the rubric (e.g., for Language Arts, "read and recognize literature as an expression of human experience"), a description of the Performance Standard (e.g., 4 = exemplary, 3 = proficient, 2 = progressing, 1 = not meeting the standards), teacher and parent comments, and a plan for meeting the standard.

Task Force

A temporary grouping of people, formed for the purpose of implementing, evaluating, analyzing, investigating, or solving a specific problem in the establishment of educational standards.

Validity

A reflection of the intended measure. Validity means that we are testing what we think we are testing.

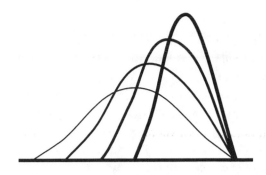

Bibliography

Baron, J.B. & Wolf, D.P. (Eds.). (1996). *Performance-based student assessment: Challenges and possibilities.* Chicago: University of Chicago Press.

Center on Learning Assessment and School Structure [CLASS]. (1995). *CLASS Summer Institute on Assessment Reform.* Princeton, NJ: CLASS. (**Note:** To order this publication, contact: CLASS, 648 the Great Road, Princeton, NJ 08540.)

Cobb, N. (Ed.). (1994). *The future of education: Perspectives on national standards in America.* New York: The College Board.

Crocker, L. & Algina, J. (1986). *Introduction to classical and modern test theory.* New York: Holt, Rinehart and Winston.

Daggett, W.R. & Kruse, B. (1997). *Education is not a spectator sport.* Schenectady, NY. Leadership Press.

Damon, W. (1995). *Great expectations. Overcoming the culture of indulgence in our homes and schools.* New York: Free Press Paperbacks.

Darling-Hammond, L., Einbender, L., & Frelow, F. et al. (1993, October). *Authentic assessment in practice: A collection of portfolios, performance tasks, exhibitions, and documentation.* New York: National Center for Restructuring Education, Schools, and Teaching.

Educational Testing Service[ETS]. (1995). *Performance assessment: Different needs, difficult answers.* Princeton, NJ: ETS. (**Note:** To order this publication, contact: ETS, 1425 Lower Ferry Rd., Trenton, NJ 08618, phone 609-771-7670, fax 609-771-7906.)

Gardner, H. (1991). *The unschooled mind: How children think and how schools should teach.* New York: Basic Books.

Goleman, D. (1995). *Emotional intelligence. Why it can matter more than IQ.* New York, Bantam Books.

Goodlad, J.I. (1990). *Teachers for our nation's schools.* San Francisco: Jossey-Bass.

Hirsch, Jr. E.D. (1996). *The schools we need and why we don't have them.* New York: Doubleday.

Hanson, F.A. (1993). *Testing testing: Social consequences of the examined life.* Berkeley: University of California Press. (**Note:** This offers a fascinating historical critique of tests.)

Howard, R. (Ed.). (1993). *The learning imperative: Managing people for continuous innovation.* Boston: Harvard Business School.

Howe, K.R. (1994, November). Standards, assessment, and equality of educational opportunity. *Educational Researcher, 23*(8), 27-32.

Keillor, G.A. (1974). *Prairie home companion.* Minneapolis, MN: American Public Radio Network. (**Note:** Garrison Keillor first began this broadcast in 1974. This program can presently be heard throughout the US on National Public Radio Stations.)

LeMahieu, P.G., Gitomer, D.H., & Eresh, J.T. (Fall 1995). Portfolios in large-scale assessment: Difficult but not impossible. *Educational Measurement: Issues and Practice,* 11-16.

Marsh, H.W. (1984). Students' evaluations of university teaching: Dimensionality, reliability, validity, potential biases, and utility. *Journal of Educational Psychology, 76,* 707-54.

Marzano, R.J. & Kendall, J.S. (1996). *A comprehensive guide to designing standards-based districts, schools and classrooms.* Alexandria, VA: Association for Supervision and Curriculum Development.

Miller, B. & Singleton, L. (1995, January). *Preparing citizens: Linking authentic assessment and instruction in civic/law-related education.* Boulder, CO: Social Science Education Consortium.

Mitchell, R. (1996). *Front-end alignment: Using standards to steer education change—A manual for developing standards.* Washington, DC: The Education Trust. (**Note:** To order this 58 page book, contact: Publications Orders Desk, American Association for Higher Education, One Dupont Circle, NW, Suite 360, Washington, DC, 20036-1110, Telephone 202-293-6440, ext. 11, Fax 202-293-0073.)

Mitchell, R. (1992). *Testing for learning: How new approaches to evaluation can improve american schools.* New York: The Free Press.

Mitchell, R., Willis, M., & The Chicago Teachers Union Quest Center. (1995). *Learning in overdrive: Designing curriculum, instruction, and assessment from standards.* Golden, CO: North American Press.

National Educational Goals Panel. (1995). *The national education goals report: Building a nation of learners.* Washington, D.C.: U.S. Government Printing Office.

Naftulin, D.H., Ware, J.E., & Donnelly, F.A. (1973). The Doctor Fox lecture: A paradigm of educational seduction. *Journal of Medical Education, 48,* 630-635.

Perkins, D. (1995). *Outsmarting IQ: The emerging science of learnable intelligence.* New York: The Free Press.

Powell, B. & Steelman, L.C. (Spring 1996). Bewitched, bothered, and bewildering: The use and misuse of state SAT and ACT scores. *Harvard Educational Review, 61*(1), 27-59.

Ravitch, D. (1995). *National standards in American education (a citizens guide).* Washington, D.C.: Brookings Institution Press.

Rothman, R. (1995). *Measuring up: Standards, assessment, and school reform.* San Francisco: Jossey-Bass.

Shepard, L.A. & Bliem, C.L. (1995, November). Parents' thinking about standardized tests and performance assessments. *Educational Researcher,* 25-32.

Slavin, R. (1994). *Educational psychology* (4th ed.). Boston: Allyn and Bacon.

Sykes, C.J. (1995). *Dumbing down our kids: Why American children feel good about themselves but can't read, write, or add.* New York: St. Martin's Press.